Coming Back to Life

PRAISE FOR
Coming Back to Life

"In *Coming Back to Life,* Rebeccah Silence shares her gut-wrenching challenges and miraculous overcomings. She lovingly imparts wisdom and insights born of experience as a world-class healing leader and offers unique and powerful tools for your positive growth. I've known Rebeccah for a long time. She longs for a world of love and dreams coming true, realized one act, person, or relationship at a time. With this writing, she gently but firmly encourages us to heal our trauma and pain so that we commit to living our most inspired life. I wholeheartedly recommend this book—and taking its advice to heart."

—**Ken Streater,** bestselling author of *Be the Good* and *The Gift of Courage*

"*Coming Back to Life* is the book that the world needs in this moment. It will illuminate what has been invisibly holding you back and give you a clear path to feeling good and getting what you want. If you are ready to release the suffering and step into possibility, Rebeccah is here as a trusted coach, guide, and friend to take a stand for your healing. The spiritual medicine offered in this book will open your heart, transform your pain, and give you a whole new relationship with life itself. You will be moved by Rebeccah's incredible story, inspired by the inner reflections she offers you, and changed by the journey she leads you through in this powerful work. The world is about to be deeply moved by Rebeccah's gripping testimony of coming back to life—make sure you don't miss the miracles waiting for you inside!"

—**Stephen Lovegrove,** America's Life Coach

"*Coming Back to Life* is a must-read if you're ready to take your life and power back. Rebeccah's story will help you connect to your story and uncover the patterns that have been blocking you. She provides real solutions to feeling better about any past traumas and offers us hope-filled possibilities that are absolutely life-changing."

—**Heather Burgett,** award-winning publicist and visibility expert

"*Coming Back to Life*: a story of triumph and victory. Rebeccah Silence, gifted coach, speaker, facilitator, and author, offers her experience through stories, coaching, and challenges of living when all seems lost. The lessons and stories in this book will move you to believe, get up, step forward, and free yourself as you free your emotions. I have been blessed to know and work with Rebeccah for over a decade. Witnessing her commitment to life, love, and people is a breath of fresh air in tough times. Allow Rebeccah to lift your spirits and share with you (from being there) what it takes to truly live!"

—**Heather Steele,** founder of Integrative Holistic Coaching

A ROADMAP TO HEALING
FROM PAIN TO CREATE
THE LIFE YOU WANT

Coming Back to Life

REBECCAH SILENCE, MS

Health Communications, Inc.
Boca Raton, Florida

www.hcibooks.com

**Library of Congress Cataloging-in-Publication Data
is available through the Library of Congress**

© 2022 Rebeccah Silence

ISBN-13: 978-07573-2446-8 (Paperback)
ISBN-10: 07573-2446-0 (Paperback)
ISBN-13: 978-07573-2447-5 (ePub)
ISBN-10: 07573-2447-9 (ePub)

HCI, its logos, and marks are trademarks of Health Communications, Inc.

Publisher: Health Communications, Inc.
301 Crawford Blvd., Suite 200
Boca Raton, FL 33432-1653

Cover, interior design and formatting by Larissa Hise Henoch

To my husband, Mark, and to my daughters,
Madison Louise and Seneca RoseMarie,
who taught me how to love and have
made my life a dream come true.

Contents

Chapter Five

Chapter Six

Chapter Seven

Chapter Eight

Chapter Nine

Chapter Ten

Chapter Eleven

Preface

WHY THIS BOOK

We are in an epidemic.

Now more than ever before the world needs healing, emotional healing. Mindset work and inspiration are not enough to help people emotionally heal. Millions of Americans are self-medicating, suffering from mental health diagnoses, and are not getting the support that they need to function, heal, and lead healthy lives. *Coming Back to Life* is a road map that offers real tools, strategies, and support that will allow readers to get to the root of their pain patterns, while also giving them hope, encouragement, and access to the light at the end of the dark tunnel that they may be stuck in or living in.

This book is timely and, I believe, could save lives. My expertise as a coach and practitioner of Emotional Healing Release work with clients and audiences for more than fifteen years needs to be given to the world en masse. I have lived through hell as a survivor of childhood sexual abuse, domestic violence, and cancer. I have beaten the odds. Now it's time to teach people how to stay in the game of their lives and how to pick up the pieces so that they can live healthy, happy, and free. The goal is to help people see how their unhealed past is impacting their lives and the experiences they are having today. From there they learn steps to begin to heal and confront unhealed emotional wounds so that they can design a clear and healed future for their life. We can't change circumstances, diagnoses, or make anything that hurt us go away after the fact, but we can learn to feel how we want to feel and live how we want to live now.

The problem with the personal growth and mental wellness industry is that it's built on statistics and is largely dependent on people consuming information and being dependent on therapists, coaches, and mentors, instead of learning how to navigate and trust their own internal guidance system. While there are many excellent therapists out there, I work with people every day who have been in therapy for decades, working on the same problems. Then they work with me, and in one coaching intensive they heal that thing they thought they couldn't heal and would have to live with forever, and then we're onto the next issue. I've created the Healing Is Possible movement and am writing this book so that people can pick and choose what they want for themselves instead of buying into statistics and relying on what someone else tells them they need. No one knows what other people are going through or what they need. My goal is to teach each reader of this book how to connect to that part of themselves that knows themselves. That trusts themselves. That loves themselves and their lives. And that has the power to live fully.

I'm not knocking therapy and yet I do think that the therapeutic model is flawed. I offer tools and strategies and insight that allow for true breakthroughs, meaning life is never the same again and pain patterns are absolutely healed. People are drowning and this book is a life raft. The key differentiator in my work with people is that they are the expert. They become their own healer. And they are already healed and whole; they just may not believe or know it, yet. I've beaten the statistical odds and so can anyone who wants to, or, at the very least, they can die trying.

I admit that this book doesn't solve or heal everything. It does, however, create an opening to possibility and life. My courses, retreats, podcasts, and coaching services are there to support people deeper after they read the book if they so desire. The tools, strategies, and methodologies that I offer are proven to work, heal and change lives, starting with mine. *How you feel is 100 percent based on how healed your past is.* You never have to feel powerless again and that is a promise.

Introduction

The darkness is real—and so is the light. I would know. I know horror. I know terror. I know what it means to think I'm going to die and defy the odds. I know how to live with the pain, to endure, and to live in spite of the hell that I was waking up to and going to bed with every day. Childhood trauma and sexual abuse that began when I was only four years old left me lost, hopeless, and in the deepest hell of shame, for decades. I thought I was too much. I thought it was my fault. I thought I could have done things differently to change people and outcomes. Very young I took on the job that it was my responsibility to have been the one to stop the abuse cycle that I grew up in. I thought if I could be good, make a difference, and make others nicer, then my family's pain would stop. As a kid I would try not to move in bed thinking that maybe, just maybe, if I could hold still and stay awake, I wouldn't get hurt that night or the next day. I would wake up in the morning and plaster a fake smile on my face and not talk, because I had decided that talking could and would make everything worse. Then I would go through the motions, a shell of a person. I have been a martyr. A victim. A lost soul. And have emerged victorious. Who knew that childhood trauma could heal? I didn't know if it could or not. But I had a dream that it could and, for me, that dream came true. This book is for those of you who want to defeat your emotional pain and personal hell so that you can emerge victorious, and finally live free.

Who knew that the endurance and grit that came out of me because of my tormented childhood would save my life at thirty-four years old when I was pregnant and diagnosed with stage 3 cancer? More on this later, but my body has taken the beatings and has held me together. These eyes have seen and cried enough tears to drown my past. I've cried through every moment I thought would kill me. I've rocked the boat over and over again to prove that I could still stand and land on my feet. My body went from my worst enemy to being my best friend and a tool of healing. It doesn't lie, ever. Yours doesn't either. It's been a long road, a hard road, and a painful road. A road so painful that I've been suicidal, on antidepressants, and ready to give up more times than I can count. But I didn't give up. I tell myself every day, *It's okay to want to quit; just don't.* There have been moments of darkness but I've learned how not to be afraid of the dark. I want to teach you how to be the electricity and lightning that will jump-start your life and your next season of life. I've learned that healing doesn't have to be a long, hard, and painful road. It can happen so fast—if we're willing to move through resistance and commit fully to being who it takes to create the lives we long for.

My life has been a series of fortunate events that have shaped me into a woman who is unshakably whole, unstoppable, and madly in love with life and people. I live like I'm going to live. I want the most out of my life. I want my life to be clear, healed and inspired—and it is. I want this for all of you, too, if you want it. You can heal because you can change your mind; change your mind about who you think you are, who you have been, and what you believe is possible for you. You can heal because you can open your heart to life in all of its moments and seasons. You can heal because you can choose who you want to be and become that person. When you do this, you get free, instantly. Then you, one single person making a commitment to healing, can change everything for everyone you will ever meet.

Healing is a spiritual process that will give you every reason not to take it on; take it on anyway.

YOU NEVER HAVE TO FEEL POWERLESS AGAIN.

YOU NEVER HAVE TO LIVE WITH YOUR PAST HAUNTING YOU AGAIN.

YOU NEVER HAVE TO LIVE WITHOUT HAVING YOUR NEEDS MET—EVER AGAIN.

Believe it or not, achieving goals, getting what you want, and creating results won't change how you feel. Emotionally healing, releasing, and re-committing to your life *will* change how you feel and will give you your life back. And then you get to create your dreams along the way, enjoying the fruits of your labor.

In this book you'll learn how to confront your pain, head-on, so that you can be happy. You may think you are avoiding confrontation, but really you are avoiding being happy. Life doesn't have to be so hard, so painful, so monotonous and so overwhelming, when you have all you need to live. I have never met a person who didn't think that they are too much. I have also never met a person who also didn't think that they aren't enough. We make it about our insecurities. We know our stories, what we've lived through and survived, and what we believe about our lives and our worth. We make our way through life surviving instead of being alive, living in spite of our heartbreak instead of healing our heart break. And we don't have to.

There's pain you can see and there's pain you can't see. There's pain you can touch and pain that you can't. When you take the meaning out of the pain, and see it as just where you are still unhealed, you can *do* something about it. When you make pain and suffering mean something *about* you, then you're less alive. This book looks at what is possible from multiple angles so that you can live, fully alive, for the rest of your life. Many of us are carrying around more upset and suffering than we want to be carrying. You wouldn't believe how much junk is buried in our bodies and in our very *cells*. We can't "think" our pain into thriving. We stuff our truth and carry stress and dumb ourselves down, which feeds the death of our souls. Are you aware of how much you are contributing to your emotional and spiritual death? There has to be a better way. And there is. Our pain protects us. It's there because we feed it. In this book let's explore together how, where and when we lost ourselves, and let's explore what we can do about that now. Let's begin to look forward to being alive. PSA: You are not broken. You get to feel how you want to feel, free and fulfilled. Before you make your problems about your circumstances, consider that the heartbreak you carry can heal and you can be reborn if you will just choose to live fully.

Your heart will break. It did break and it can also heal. Your broken heart doesn't have to be the boss anymore. We all look for evidence to prove our broken heart is right, but at what cost? The only medicine that can actually heal your broken heart is you loving you. Cheesy, maybe, but you honoring you. You listening to and caring about you. That's a life. Your heart needs you, not the world, to be different. Your pain is your heartbreak. And your heartbreak is the gateway to your soul breaking through so that you can play, laugh, listen, and experience pure joy and bliss. When we were kids, we didn't get to vote on our parents' choices and we got hurt. No one comes out of their childhood unscathed. Every child gets hurt; no one is immune. It's no one's fault. It happened to our parents too.

You'll hear parts of my story in these pages so I can paint a vivid picture of what is possible for you. Vicious childhood abuse broke my heart; then I decided absolutely for decades that love and life meant a broken heart. Love and heartbreak, in my mind, went together. This became a death sentence since, as we can't live without food, we can't live without love either. This book is about my story through heartbreak and the weight I've carried and eventually let go of, through emotional healing. Healing is possible. This has been true for me and I absolutely believe that it's true for you as well.

There are details here that I won't go into, not because I'm ashamed or because I want to protect the predators. The stories I've chosen are exactly right for this book, and it's a young girl's memory of events that shaped her. Other people may have, and I am certain do have, different versions of some of these stories. Other people have also been impacted. The details don't matter anyway; it's the aftermath and the healing cycle after that makes the difference. I'm going to teach you the cycle to healing that will help you come back to life. If my life and story can help my readers, then it's all been worth it.

Imagine a world where we all became who we could become. A world where we all meet the toughest, strongest, and highest versions of ourselves. You coming back to life is the solution and, in this book, one chapter at a time, I'll teach you how to experience and move through darkness into more possibility and light, regardless of circumstances that you have survived or that you are facing now. There is a way out and the way out is *you*. You can't skip the part where you recognize that you will have to let go of who you thought you were to become the version of you that it takes to have the life you want, and that knowing is how you can begin to come back to life.

Let's face it. People are suffering and that could include you. Today we all have a glorious opportunity to look at and reflect on how we have been living. Having survived your life so far along with a global pandemic, you'll discover that the gift of clarity and vision and an opportunity to create the life and lifestyle that you truly want is right here, hidden in plain sight. If you don't want to live the way you've been living, *then start again.* Are you ready to stop letting your past bleed into your future? Are you ready to get beyond survival mode and to begin to live the way you want to live? Be honest. Are you living the way you want to be living? Are you carrying suffering, heartbreak, emotional pain, stress and worry with you in your days, weeks, and months right now? That can all change and fast.

After more than twenty years of personal growth work, including participating in more than 100 seminars and surviving my way through childhood abuse, eating disorders, depression, suicidal ideation, domestic violence, financial ruin, cancer, and so much more, I'm here to tell you that *healing is possible* and I can show you how to begin to get free and how to heal through being stuck—and leave your pain behind. It's not an easy journey but it can be simple and it's so worth it! I wasn't supposed to make it through my past, statistically speaking, but I did and you can too. Screw statistics. Take on healing. Take on learning what it means to take your life back so that you can be the person that you are meant to be. When we're being authentic and living how we want to live, nothing can threaten or harm who we really are ever again.

Let's create a healed future now for you. You are worth it and your family could use a healed version of you, I promise, not to mention the world. In these chapters, my road map to freedom is yours to use anytime you want to. You get this book for life. More importantly, reading this book can give you your life back. The time is now. The years 2020 and 2021 have shown us how precious life is and how fast it can all change. Now is your opportunity to be the catalyst in your life of the healing and change that you have been longing for. Give up going to bed longing for a different life, and create the life of your dreams. Now. I'm honored to be your guide on this healing journey. You don't want to miss one word. It's time to break up with survival mode. Healing is possible. Join me now. Let's begin!

Chapter One

THE CAR RIDE

Authenticity is a game many of us get scared to play but it's the only game worth playing.

We are going to my grandmother's house for Sunday dinner. Just a regular Sunday, except that it isn't. I'm in the passenger seat, sixteen years old, and in love with my boyfriend. He's by far the best part of my life. I've discovered my sexuality, and I'm like a tigress on the hunt. I can't wait to see him again, and it's like I'm addicted. Out of nowhere, my aunt says to me, "Well, we know he doesn't want you for your body," and my life as I know it is over. I will never be the same again. The words play on repeat in my head: "Well, we know he doesn't want you for your body." I'm devastated, but even worse, I believe *her*. I thought my boyfriend and I were madly in love. I thought that he thought my body was beautiful. He tells me all the time, and I desperately want to believe that he can't get enough of me. I lost myself that day. I sold out. I gave me up. It is decided, like an oath, that I am not enough and that something is very, very wrong with me. Her words sting, but I take them in like water on a hot day.

I needed my boyfriend's love. I needed to see his actions as love, and to hear his words as love. He told me daily how he felt about me and how I looked through his eyes and I would listen, taking it all in like a lullaby. My aunt's seven stingingly painful words, "He doesn't want you for your body," sliced through my heart and my life changed forever.

I decided once and for all that I was unhealed, that something was wrong with me. I was too fat, too much, too unlovable, and too not enough. My boyfriend was my sense of security and in some ways he had even become part of my identity. I thought he loved me. I thought he thought I was beautiful. This car ride became the car ride of my life. This was when I believed someone else's words and stopped believing my fantasy romance and life was a possibility. I was crushed. I loved my boyfriend. He was my great first love. I poured my soul into him day after day for more than five years. When his eyes would find mine, nothing could hurt me. When his lips touched mine I knew, because I had to know, that I was somebody worth loving. His hands held me together, when every day back then I felt like I was one breath away from falling apart. I had made up and believed for the first time in my life that I was loved, wanted, safe, and someone's everything.

Then my world, along with my vision of love, fell apart, all of a sudden, because of something one person said. In that car, my experience of my body, myself and love, changed in that one moment. The car ride from hell. I couldn't get out of that car for decades. My need to fit in with my family and ultimately what I thought the world wanted me to be took over. Honoring, respecting, and loving me as I was every day just was not an option. Can you relate? Life stayed this way for years. I thought it was because I *couldn't* get out of that car. The real truth was that I *would not* get out of the car—until I finally did. At sixteen, my heart was broken. I decided, absolutely, that my body was putting me in the red, at a deficit. My body became my fatal flaw on winding upstate New York backroads. What I wouldn't give to be able to knock on the window of that car and give those two women a pep talk. I may not have the ability to go back in time, but as I write to you, I am imagining myself, as I am now, knocking on the sixteen-year-old me's window and asking her to roll it down, or better yet, step out of the car. I would tell her, "I have some things you need to hear before you turn into an anorexic who loathes yourself. Before you go on living in such a way that you are living in spite of your body, living into unwellness and the opposite of healing and being fully alive." Men became a scapegoat. My first love didn't stand a chance. Men were never going to love me for my body and I would hate them for it. Abusive men became my drug of choice after this. I wish I could have looked into sixteen-year-old Rebeccah's eyes and said, "Be careful. You are never going to be too much body or person for any man. Watch out for mean women talking shit about your body, or any woman's body for that matter. Have some self-respect and know that when you marry the guy that gets you pregnant at twenty-three, who called you names like twat, cunt, slut, and whore almost daily, who cheated on you, hit you, and eventually financially devastated you, it wasn't because of your body, it was because you were unhealed, not believing that healing is possible. Before you decide that everything that will go wrong in your life is because you are too fat, please listen up. Rebeccah, you are not, and never ever were, too fat. Your only problem is that you lost your voice somewhere along the way. You lost yourself when you decided that you were too fat." This is me talking now to sixteen-year-old me and to all of you. We are not too much or not enough; we are unhealed and yet we are extraordinary. Let's give all of ourselves to ourselves in this precious lifetime. It's time to come back to life. We got hurt. And then we insist that we will get hurt again so the only choice is to shut our hearts down. This is the beginning of dis-ease and toxicity that keeps us unhealed. It's the beginning of the slow death of our souls.

I'm about to drop a bomb on you. Being in emotional pain has nothing to do with the events that have happened in your past. The emotional pain you carry is because you won't heal through the stuck emotions and beliefs that you made up about yourself and what is possible for you based on those events. And worse, the age you got stuck in is the age you regress to every time a similar trigger gets activated.

For example, if at age sixteen I decided I am only going to be loved in spite of my body and I decide that I am too fat, and carry shame about that, every time I'm trying to get love in spite of my body I am sixteen, carrying stuck rage, fear and grief that bleeds out all over anyone in my path, especially the poor bastards trying to love me. This was me.

Really it all boiled down to a worthiness issue. If I don't heal through all this emotional cancer and gunk then I'm not worthy, that's that, and life will remind me over and over and over again, which is exactly what happened in my life for decades. Can you see how, as long as the teenage Rebeccah was in charge, I was basically screwed and screwed up?

This is how it works. I say "I'm not worthy," and it's so. Or, I'm too fat, I'm not good enough, I'm stupid, I can't do it, I should just give up, I'm a failure, I'm a joke, I'm going to get abandoned, I'm a victim, I'm an embarrassment, I want too much, I shouldn't talk, I could go on and on. This is how pain patterns are born.

What's yours? What's the pain pattern taking up so much space in your life right now? Find it. Write it down. This is where we start to get real, raw and messy, together so that the healing can begin. Our pain patterns become a life sentence, an identity that holds us hostage and suffocates the life out of us. My big question to you is, why does it have to get so painful before we listen to our emotions and do the work to heal so that we can meet ourselves?

Please, I beg you to hear me, you do not need a crisis or to blow up your life so that you can get free. Chances are you will just repeat patterns with new characters in different costumes until you have done the emotional work to heal, repair, and reinvent.

Now I have a hard ask of you. *Please,* unless you are in a dangerous or abusive environment where your safety is at risk, do not make any major life changes until you've finished this book and gotten support from a professional. If your safety is at risk, get help right away. And keep reading for more on how to heal emotionally while you take your life back.

YOU ARE NOT ALONE, SEEK HELP

National Suicide Prevention Lifeline:
suicidepreventionlifeline.org, 988

National Domestic Violence Hotline:
1-800-799-7233, or text START to 88788

This book isn't the whole answer but it is a beginning. Find a mirror to look into. I want you to look in that mirror and make eye contact, first with you, the adult, in charge. Then with that inner child. Take a breath and say out loud, "We are in this together and we're going to heal together." Then make a promise to yourself, out loud, that you won't blow your whole life up but you will be the difference maker that starts from where you are and is committed to healing your future and your life. Congratulations! You are about to go deeper than you've ever gone so that you can soar and live, alive, and in powerful leadership.

If any part of me sharing my story can help you love yourself more, and let go of the "weight" that you carry, then it's all been worth it. I have lived under a cloud of self- hatred and to me there is nothing worse. Cancer is better than self-loathing and I actually know that for a fact. It's time for the hopeless conversations with ourselves and with each other to get put to bed. It's time for us to win in the bodies we have, in the circumstances we have, and in the lives we have. It's time to change our minds about what is possible. It's time to flip the switch inside of you to turn on your power.

So, all this sounds good but how do you turn you on when you feel that it's impossible or carry unimaginable pain? Big scary question, right? What I gained from that fateful car ride was the cost of buying into and believing someone else's truth over my own. I know that I am living a lie when I'm in hell. You are living a lie when you suffer, even a little bit.

It's time to get real.

Authenticity is a game many of us get scared to play but it's the only game worth playing. Life can become, if you will be brave, a journey back to you being you. Authenticity is a journey of connection back to our souls. It's important to note that like enlightenment, authenticity and what's authentic to us will change, and that's okay. We just have to stay honest with ourselves moment to moment.

You'll know that you are being and living inauthentically if you feel "off" at all. Sometimes it's a whisper, sometimes it's physical pain. Off is off, it's real and it hurts. Unless we are turned all the way on, on a soul level, we don't work and feel awful! It's time to turn it all the way up, even if you are scared. Anything or anyone that goes away because you turn you all the way on and all the way up is no longer serving you or your life. The harder part is you may feel like you don't know how or who you are.

So, how do you turn you on and all the way up if you don't know who you are? Ask yourself, *What is true for me now, what do I want now, what am I needing to let go of now, what am I making room for now?* Then listen. That's enough. The answers will come. From there, keep breathing and keep trying again and again. Just keep coming back to your breath, your heartbeat, and *listen*. Breathe and align. Breathe and align.

What would it be like to give yourself permission to listen to you so that you meet you? If you are stumped on where to even begin listening to yourself, start with listening to your body. The best, most beautiful and brilliant part of you is talking 24/7, no matter how much emotional pain you are in. But are you listening? We get surrounded by "upsets." We take in our stress and our suffering and play with and roll around in "it" when we stop connecting and listening to ourselves. Listen to your body and it will give you access to your soul, no matter what size, situation, or circumstance you are in today. It's time to take your life back. Your body knows and it will guide you.

You can't take your life back without your body. If you won't align with your body, you can't be free. Freedom is your right. Inspired and authentic living is your right, regardless of your struggle. No one can take the opportunity of your life away from you. No one can lead your life except you. And you can't lead your life without your body.

Are you ready for the two questions that you can ask yourself *anytime* in any situation to take your power back? These two questions can be game changers:

HOW DO I FEEL IN THIS MOMENT RIGHT NOW?

HOW DO I *WANT* TO FEEL RIGHT NOW?

Really! Try it. Ask *and then* listen to your body for the answers. Let it tell you how it feels and what it wants until it feels like your favorite outfit that is just the right size. Then let this next question give you direction on your next right step for you:

WHAT DO I WANT?

This question is so simple and yet it's everything. Only you can decide where you are headed. You always have control over that question and you have that answer in you. You can, and are capable of withstanding any storm that comes your way. What life storm have you not survived as you read these pages? Exactly. You've only survived all of them! When you're certain of where you are headed and listening to how you want to feel and what you want, then all you have to do is keep putting one foot in front of the other until you cross the finish line. Just make sure that your feet are still moving toward your dreams— and you're on your way. It's not another person or system or situation that's in your way, the pain, or anything else that's your problem, it's you being uncertain of where you're headed. When we know who we are, where we are headed and why, we become unstoppable. It's time to cut through the pain. Part of cutting through is asking these three questions. From there we can begin getting out of life on autopilot and reacting and letting go of life as we think it's supposed to be.

What so many of us do is focus on our pain as the problem. As cliché as it is, when we focus on what we don't want we have no access to what we do want. Start paying attention to how much you are focusing on what you don't want. How many hours a day? When you catch it, ask yourself what you want instead.

I get it. You might not know. So many of us have buried our internal guidance system down as deeply as we could. How easily we forget that we are the solution to everything in our lives. We forget that we in fact do know the way back to ourselves on a soul level.

How are you doing so far? Are you more awake? More conscious and more joyful at the possibility yet? Even a smidge?

Freedom is taking the lead in what takes care of and honors you. Other people's limitations and fear do not have to determine your fate and neither does your pain. What I mean is, don't restrict your possibilities based on other people's fear, limitations or obstacles, or your own suffering. Get out of the conversation with yourself about what you think you can and can't have because of where you are now.

Living in a world of "I can't" leads to emotional, mental, spiritual, and physical hell. Your body has been through enough. You have been through enough. Breathe that in and say it out loud: "I have been through enough."

It's not about your past, your story or your struggle. It's about letting go of anything that isn't you that you are allowing to shape the experience you are having of your life. Abuse, weight, cancer, disease, your finances, your relationship status, are all real and metaphors for where we are unhealed and what we carry around every minute of our days.

We see through filters of fear. Be the person who sets yourself free and see the "you" under the pain. It's time to let that person out. You have the key to unlock your soul. Only you. And you can do it no matter what situation you find yourself in right now. I am not unworthy, and neither are you.

It's only because there once was a moment where you decided the world couldn't handle you that you stopped shining bright. It wasn't the world. *You couldn't handle the world's reaction to you or your fear about how the world would react if you were honest.* That's what happened. And that only happened because you were young.

I remember playing basketball with my father, who was my favorite parent, when I was four. I was asking all kinds of questions. I wanted to know. I wanted to learn. I wanted to understand. I have no idea what I was even asking about. I just remember shooting the basketball and him saying to me, "Rebeccah, why do you ask so many questions?"—and then walking away. I was gut punched. I didn't understand. What I didn't know then is that he was probably hungover and his bad mood wasn't about me. But at four, I took in self-doubt and drank it down like it was a spoonful of medicine. What I digested about myself in that moment was a belief that I asked too many questions and that made people go away. I made my inquisitive nature a bad thing about myself when in fact it's one of my proudest assets.

Are you starting to see how easy it is to stop ourselves from fully being seen, heard, and loved for who we are authentically? One moment, that's it, is when you got hurt. The event happened and you made up a story, a meaning about you, that hurt and then you got stuck there. One moment at a time. Your heart broke. When was it? What was your first heartbreak? How old were you? What happened? What did you decide about you and what was possible for you? Take some time to journal this. I know it might feel like a lot. You can go here. Just please promise yourself that you aren't going to go off the deep end as you go here. And no self-medicating or feeding your inner victim as you go here. The goal is healing. The goal is to come out the other side. The goal is to not let the dark win. As you begin to get real about your heartbreak the light starts to shine in, from within.

I am *not* sorry your heart got broken. I'm not saying this to be mean. I am saying this because I am proud of you. I want you to see that the world needs you living as YOU. Your adapting down instead of up, is 100 percent on you. The world can't force you to not show up for your own life.

I know it hurt and probably still hurts. But will you please stop taking your hurt out on your body and your life, on those you love and on the world? You living with a broken heart means that you loved. You went for it. You were willing to risk losing something or someone you loved. That loss is just the end of a moment of your life, it's not the end of your life. There will always be another end of the line but it doesn't mean your life is over unless you decide that it does. There will also be a new beginning for you with every end. Yes, for you. The beginning can feel like magic. The ends aren't the end of the magic. They make way for new, more, miracles and rebirth.

We have *all* had our hearts break. Then we forgot to make room for the new, for more, and rebirth. *Oops.* You carry the weight of your broken heart and the weight of you not putting yourself out there again and it's killing your soul and your spirit. It's time to put yourself out there again. The more you live, the more of a guarantee that you will experience more beginnings and more endings and living through both, over and over again, brings more life, in all of its messy and gorgeous splendor.

Your soul would really love for you to risk keeping your heart open. And your life depends on it. No one ever felt light and free with a closed down protected heart. That's heavy and sad. It's lonely too. Feel it out. Feel it out. Feel it and you will heal and love again. Say it out loud, right now, "It's safe to feel. I can feel to heal." My experience is one of my heart being in my hands, held out to the lives and world in front of me as an offering. Every time I want to protect my heart I know it's time to give even more of my heart to whoever or whatever I am facing.

What you may already know or possibly didn't realize is that you are carrying weight that is emotional. It's safe to let it out. You already survived. Now you are an adult and you get to choose. No more waiting. No more denying. No more sacrificing your body, mind and soul. The cost is too much. It's too heavy. You can be free. But you've got to be willing to face your pain to release it.

You are not too messed up to be who you are on a soul level. I hope you are feeling me and hearing these words in your heart. The time we have is the time we have. Life isn't about the moments we want, it's about the moments we have. Are you going to keep spending your life disrespecting your life? We don't know how much time we're given, but we do have the body and life that we were given.

Starting now, what will you do with it? What will you put it through, now that you are back in charge of it? For some of us in our younger or more asleep years, we didn't have or feel like we had control over our bodies or our lives. But we do. We certainly do. It can be scary to face leading ourselves in our one body out of the darkness we may be feeling or living in. I've been there.

Patterns repeat until they heal. The car ride took me, buckled up and buckled in on many more iterations of heartbreak. Until I decided to get out of that car and later off of the floor.

THE FLOOR

It feels as if the walls are closing in as I'm face-down on the bathroom floor, crying. It's an ugly, primal cry and I don't even care that my mouth is on the tile. I've forgotten everything except that it's time to go, and I can no longer pretend this is the life I want. It's a dark time and I am in love, again. I think he is, too. But this life is not safe. There is alcohol, violence, and so many lies. The biggest lie is with me, though.

Day after day I wear a brave face and try to pretend like I have the perfect life. My mind tells me that my body is rocking, my kid is perfect, my husband is hot and funny and making a success of himself.

It's all a lie. We are miserable and Lord, are there skeletons in the closet. I try to keep the skeletons at bay, while I become a skeleton myself. I am a shell of me. I am a liar. I am "eating" my truth, my circumstances, and now it's so bad and so loud that I take my child and leave. I never thought I would get divorced but that's what's happening. I can't tell whose decision the divorce is at first but it doesn't matter. I am leveled. The stone floor in my house soaks up an ocean of tears. I am so thin and for days I can't get off the floor. I just keep crying. The tears won't stop.

But I'm waking up to the cost of fake. I am so thin and at the same time I'm the heaviest I've ever been. My friends shock me when I tell them about the divorce and they are not at all surprised. They want to help me move out ASAP and orchestrate the whole thing. I will never forget this time, being moved out of my house by my friends. I was all unpacked, set up and moved into my new apartment in less than four hours. I was so embarrassed telling my friends the truth but they are supportive and grateful that I am leaving. I can't believe it. I had thought that I had everyone fooled. I was happy. Life was perfect. No, I was playing house and I was fake.

The gratitude I have for the women in my life holding me up, and who held me up, is immeasurable. The wake-up call of me not being nearly as great of an actress as I thought I was, hits me hard and also frees a part of my soul. It's not so bad to get found out. It doesn't make the pain of having to heal through heartbreak and start over any easier, but at least I don't have to pretend anymore.

Our heartbreaks repeat, like *Groundhog Day,* until we heal. My heartbreak on the stone floor was the same as the car ride: I'm not enough. I wasn't enough. I will be left.

My abandonment issues and yours are directly related to rejecting and abandoning ourselves. You begin to heal through abandonment when you listen to your body and your soul. When you honor and respect yourself and your life. When you stop pretending to be who you aren't and never were. Pretending feels the heaviest and we all have pretended to get by. We pretend good enough is good enough or that we are doing better than we are. We pretend and it makes us sick. I hate "Fake it until you make it." Get real and get committed instead. Then you will lose emotional weight and begin to truly heal, once and for all. Try it. My heart broke on the car ride and started to heal as I got up off the floor, got real, and got divorced.

It's time to start allowing yourself to struggle through what's in the way of your health and happiness. Where is fear running you? What are you running from? Where are you hopeless?

Some days we carry emotional weight. Some days we carry physical weight. Some days spiritual weight. Some days we feel strong. The pain is real and some days it feels like too much. But you are always stronger. You get to meet you now, with life how it is now, if you will take that challenge on.

The lies I've lived have been infinite. I'm too much has been the number one lie that I've lived. I've been and currently am, on the obesity charts. But I'm not too much or too fat to be alive. I'm not too much or too fat to be all of who I am. I'm not too much or too fat to write this book or to coach the thousands that I coach. I'm not too much or too fat to speak and share my truth, and neither are you.

Journal EXERCISE

- How do you feel about your life right now?
- How do you want to feel about your life right now?
- What was the moment where you decided the world couldn't handle you?
- Where is fear running you?
- What are you running from?
- Where are you hopeless?
- What do you want now?
- Why do you want this?
- How will it change your life to create what you want for yourself?

Chapter Two

THE MIRROR

You belong because you breathe. Your breath gives more life force to the planet. Those who step into belonging to themselves can welcome each breath no matter what they are breathing into. We belong to each other, the Earth, and God. You are a miracle and each step you take and each breath you take nurtures the planet. Your breath matters. Your life matters. When you belong to yourself you can embrace the support of others. A person who belongs to themselves and respects themselves can respect and embrace life, others, God, and the planet.

. . . And then everything changed. Seven years old is an age of playing, dreaming, and no worries. I am seven. I have a hero and her name is Nana. Nana is my favorite and I am lucky enough to have her close by. Most weekends we are together. She makes me pancakes and turns each one into whatever animal I want with a flick of her wrist. Unicorns, lions, tigers, and bears join us for breakfast every Sunday. She can do anything and I love our moments together and look forward to them all week long. I believe that I am loved and safe when I am with her. Her house is three stories tall, but I'm not allowed on the third floor. I know that I'm supposed to be by my grandmother's side all the time when I am with her. Except she is not always awake or around. I don't understand that when she's sleeping it's because she's sometimes has had too much to drink.

One day she was sleeping and I went upstairs. The man was an adult who I love so I go along because I don't want him to get mad at me. But I know my grandmother won't like this. There is yellow in the room. He starts touching me and takes my pants off. I'm confused and I am not sure what to do or what is happening. I'm scared. Then I hear my grandmother come up the stairs. She comes into the room and starts screaming. Then she grabs me by the arm and yanks me down the stairs. She takes me into the pantry. She grabs a wooden paddle that hangs on the wall. I don't see it coming. The paddle knocks the wind out of me. It hurts. I can't breathe. I don't understand. Nana is screaming while she hits me. I somehow get away. I'm in shock. I run through my tears, desperately trying to catch my breath. *What have I done? Why am I in trouble? Who is this lady and where did Nana go?* It's not fair. I'm so upset. One hand and foot at a time, I climb a tree in my favorite backyard. I decide that I'm not going to get out of this tree. It feels like I'm there for a long time but who knows how much time goes by. I can see my grandmother at the bottom of the tree. She's trying to talk me into getting down. She can't reach me which is a relief and also ter- rifying. She can't hurt me. I am scared of her and mad at her. Eventually my parents show up and take me home. I don't remember what happens next.

Soon after that day when everything changed, my grandmother passes away, suddenly. She's too young to die and I don't get to say goodbye. My parents say I am too little to go to the funeral. I'm confused and scared and sad, all over again. I don't know what to do so I shut down. I bury the grief and my spirit and I go on. I'm only seven. I decide that I'm the reason she died. *It's my fault.*

❧

This was one of my first heartbreaks. We don't want to feel heartbreak. The problem is if we don't feel it, the pain stays stuck in our veins, in our cells, and our hearts begin to close and the walls around us begin to grow. One event occurs and then we won't go for it again. One event and we choose to stop ourselves from being honest with ourselves and living fully. And the layers go deep. My grandmother was so special to me! She was my partner in crime. I associated fun with her. Then she was gone in a flash. I decided on a deep level that alone was better. This was the beginning of me rejecting and abandoning myself. Rejection is learned and I bought into this, hook, line, and sinker. At seven I believed that I was someone who would be rejected, abandoned, and unsupported. My emotional body took a huge hit at seven, literally and metaphor-ically. Rejected and shut down is a deadly combo and I turned it into a cocktail that was my go-to anytime I was upset. What's yours? The seven-year-old me got blindsided by my grandmother. In my little girl brain, she was not who I thought she was, and then she went away forever. I never "got" that I couldn't grieve or get mad about Nana beating me up severely and then dying. I tried to put on a brave face and move on and went up the metaphorical tree into la la land, alone. The pattern that was established looked like the women in my life, the ones I loved the most, died or disappeared. I then get blindsided and go dark. From there, there is no possibility. I'm alone. For decades I shoved down how furious I was and internalized my pain. Then my pain bled out all over the place, all while I was hoping no one would be able tell. Being *alone* was better than getting abused or abandoned. For much of my life I wouldn't fully let people in. My grandmother was my hero. Her beating me up and then her death broke my heart.

Our hearts break and the bottom of our lives falls out. Too often we blame the fallout and the heartbreak on a person or a situation. Then, understandably, we avoid future fallout, sometimes on purpose, and sometimes not meaning to. But if we're going to heal and grow and live, then what's no longer serving us must fall away to make room for something new. Allow the fall away so that you can get free. Courage helps us take our lives and power back. But we have to face the mirror first. When we face the mirror (that is, life as it is now) we gain the courage to freefall into our next level of a more abundant, happy, authentic life so that we can belong to ourselves again.

THE MIRROR DOESN'T LIE

The mirror helps us see. When we see, we have power. It takes courage to see what is real about how we've been living. The mirror shows us so much, including how desperate we are to fit into who we think we should be, and to other people's versions of how we should be. For as long as I can remember I have been desperate to be okay just as I am. You too? Until we are accepting and gentle with who we are, where we are, flaws and all, we will suffer. We ignore the beauty of our bodies, souls, and the beauty of life. It's critical that we face and admit where what we do goes against ourselves. We miss so many moments, don't we? How many times have I played crazy games with myself, like withholding sex unless I was a certain way, starving myself or throwing up my food unless I got results, focusing on surface issues instead of focusing on the toxicity of how I was living and the environment I was in. All because I didn't know how to get my environment, my life, set up well, for *me*.

It's time for you to put down your pain. Drop it like it's hot! It's not serving you or the life you want. We are and have everything we need to lose and let go of our unwillingness to get honest that holds us hostage. It's never been that you *can't* feel better; it's that you *won't believe* that you *can*. Why? Self-protection can have us in a permanent state of self-sacrifice, which is more hell. What I mean by self-sacrifice is sacrificing our truth. It's an illusion that it's unsafe to be all of who we are. Self-protection, self-sacrifice, and survival mode have won for long enough.

Self-sacrifice is something we all do at some point in our lives. My theory is that we self-sacrifice in an effort to not lose the people that we care about most. Abandonment is terrifying. It's purely devastating. Losing my grandmother to this day is one of the greatest devastations of my life and it came with incredible aftershock and aftermath. Shit happens and it's easy to think that if we were different maybe things would have gone differently. Spoiler alert, it happened how it happened and nothing could have changed the outcomes that hurt and broke your heart. No more adapting to trying to avoid conflict, unless you are willing to live against yourself, abandoning yourself further.

Trying to fit into a life that is not what you really want amounts to you abandoning you. *When we refuse to abandon ourselves, we can no longer be abandoned.* Have you ever considered that when we abandon ourselves and then blame the world for not loving us enough, that it's keeping us from being fully alive? To heal your abandonment issues it's you who has to take you back, no matter where you are in your life or how you are feeling about yourself and your life now. You are the one thing you've got for life. Stop abandoning you and your life the way it is now. We abandon ourselves more than we realize. It's insane. We're not insane, this way of living is. It's not worth it.

The thing about life and healing is that it's not cookie-cutter. This book isn't a guide to show you "the way." Instead, my hope is that this book will give you hope, clarity, and your own answers. I won't tell you what to do or what not to do or how to live. But I will tell you that it can and will get better and feel better when you let go of believing the lies about you that you've learned and lived, that haunt you.

TIME TO GET HONEST

My theory on why we lie to ourselves is because we don't know who we are beyond who we became to survive. We created a survival personality and decided it's who we are and who we need to be. How many days have you spent trying to be more of what you think you should be instead of being all of who you are? Being fake is making us sick and tired, heavy and empty. And we all do it. We've all played that we are less than we are and that hurts. It's easy to tell when you are fake because it hurts. It shows up like stress, suffering, upset, breakdown, and awfulness. Trying to adapt and conform, which has us dismiss who we are, puts so much pressure on our physical, mental, spiritual, and emotional spines. Eventually, the "weight" is going to start to take its toll, and eventually, it will bring you down and make you feel even worse. *We don't have to wait for life to get so painful that we are brought to our knees.* We lie because we want to believe the lies and we don't know what else to do, but denial isn't helping us get more alive or more healed.

So where do we go from here? It's time to have the courage to decide that life doesn't have to keep feeling painful. You don't have to spend your life feeding your wounds, your heartbreak, and your insecurities. Fear doesn't need to keep winning. It's possible to defy the odds. It's possible to beat your past and your pain and to live the way you want to live because you became a version of yourself beyond your survival personality that you respect, love, and value. The world is never going to value your life more than you value your life. No one can be better to you or for you than you are for yourself. What if you didn't have to stress about finding yourself or discovering who you really are? What if instead you just get to choose? Who you have been is not who you are unless you decide it is. Look in the mirror to face who you've been to help you see what you want to keep and what you are ready to transform, let go of, and step into. You can decide to be a version of yourself that you love, respect, create, and honor. Or, you can keep living lies—and missing out on your life.

OUR BEST CAN CHANGE THE WORLD

Any place we feel like the world is harming us, we are powerless and therefore we are leading in suffering instead of leading in more healing and more life. When we stop leading our own lives, being impacted by and reacting to events instead of powerfully leading at our best, we get miserable. We carry our excuses, limitations, and obstacles with us like badges of honor and repeat our past instead of designing the future of our dreams. Pain is heavy. Excuses are heavy. Struggle is heavy. What if life just wants us to live?

I know you've been heartbroken and that life has been hard in moments. Life goes our way sometimes and sometimes it doesn't. Life will go your way and it won't go your way and it won't be about you, it will just be life. But we take it personally and shut down instead of living more into our truth and leading. When life isn't going our way it feels like a breakdown. We don't want the struggle. We try to run from breakdowns. But what if the life is always giving us a hand to try and help us grow into the person we want to be? Into a higher version of ourselves? Into our best selves? All moments, even the ones that aren't feeling great, are opportunities to lighten up and live without the unnecessary weight of suffering that is suffocating the life out of us.

Authenticity is how you become your best. The fastest way that I know of to live authentically is to be willing to live and lead from where I am now, no matter what's happening. Read that again. It can seem hard to see opportunities in emotionally painful moments, but they are there. And *all painful moments* bring opportunities for more clarity, more connection, more healing, and more life. I'm not saying that all is well and that there's always a gift or good in the pain, even though that may be true. What I'm suggesting is that it's possible to lean in, and guess what? *You're* the only one who can. Needing any part of life to be different than it is or was, is what's making you want to crawl out of your skin and out of your life. It happened or it is happening—now what? What will you choose? What is your truth? What do you want your next outcome to be?

We hold so much stress in our bodies and in our brains. Chaos, life, happens all around us, all of the time, and that's not going to change any time soon. When we allow ourselves to get caught up in chaos and lose ourselves, we feel out of control. Instead of just reacting, we can choose to be the leaders of our experience, the catalyst that makes a healthier impact and models new experiences and possibilities to the world.

The practice of emotional healing is about learning how to be centered and stable even in turbulence. Every moment is another chance. Nothing has ever been a waste of your time. Please do not, as you start to connect some dots about where you are not living fully, worry about wasted time. We spend so much time worrying. It's killing your spirit and your soul. The new victory dance is to allow the worry and to move forward regardless. Instead of worrying about whatever it might be: body, time, kids, money, relationship status, sex, family, friends, career, who you think you should be, or obligations, please, let your best be enough. And now do better. Begin from where you are. Your answers are all just one solution away. The sooner you allow the struggle and face the mirror, the lighter and more alive you will feel.

THE STRUGGLE IS YOUR SOLUTION

You can get to life beyond struggle but the struggle is the gateway and solution to your freedom. Struggle is an indicator that you are not living authentically, yet. Life doesn't have to include stress and struggle as a given. Who we are when we're struggling is not who we want to be or there would be no struggle. Struggling, faking your life, and dimming yourself down is hurting and undermining you. Life is a mirror showing you where it's time to get courageous and honest. Have the courage to become the source of your own encouragement. What I mean by that is, know who you are, know that your best is enough, know your intentions, and then the world's reaction to you no longer becomes the proof the you are worthy or "on track" because you already know. All the times we wait for permission, approval, or believe what others tell us about ourselves are making us sick emotionally and physically, and yes, killing us.

What would it be like to let the world see you in all of your magnificence? Does this sound exhausting to you? Or too hard? Impossible? Do you want easy or do you want your life? None of what I'm suggesting is easy but it is simple. Who are you underneath all of your fear is the one person who has what it takes to give you your life back. I'm not trying to be harsh but someone has to say it. We hide. We retreat. We shut down our truths. We won't admit that we are not too much or that it's a lie that we aren't enough. Not being who we really are is the source of the pain in our lives. What if it's okay to acknowledge where we are lying to ourselves and to others? Every lie dims your light. Every lie undermines you. Insecurities, pleasing, and being "nice" isn't working, for any of us. Nice implies that the world can't handle your truth. You don't need to be nice. It's okay to get real and honest, and it's okay to receive acknowledgement about how wonderful and beautiful you are. I see it so much that people are willing to focus on problems while they look for their flaws or what they think is wrong with them. Why is it so much easier to take in and receive the negative feedback from the world instead of experiencing your greatness and letting the world reflect your greatness and your best back at you? If you won't take in or are needing compliments, it's making you less of who you are. Lies, cheating yourself and others, stealing time from yourself and others, and all of the times you think you "can't" are not serving you, anymore. All of the times you believed someone's insults and criticisms, including your own, are stealing your courage. Start to look for feedback that supports who you are at your best and who you are becoming. It's there as much as the painful feedback is, look for it.

Up your courage game and understand that we get to be crazy about life and each other, in the best way. Healing, inspiration, and the results we want are waiting for us. It's time. It's time to get brave enough to step into your courage so that you can love your life, in all of its moments, day in and day out, while you are still alive.

You are *not* confused. You've just been in a power struggle with life. Your childhood may have been confusing or you were getting mixed messages that had you feel like you weren't seeing what you were seeing. You weren't confused about what you saw or what happened. It's just that the people around you couldn't see what you were seeing. You were right about what you knew was possible but because your family didn't agree or didn't see *you* because of their own pain, you thought you were wrong or confused. Your truth, your power, and your greatness can never hurt anyone. It may not have been received well in childhood so your survival personality shut down. But it hurts you when you won't go all in, letting the world meet and experience all of you. And you can know that you aren't confused now and commit to a life of your best, and your truth while you only surround yourself with people that honor you at your best and want your truth. Sometimes the truth feels hard but it never is. Denying your truth is what's hard. Saying it out loud will make you lighter. Of course, not everyone will get it, want to hear it, or support you. Oh well! So what? Stop doing your life feeling so alone. Stop avoiding, especially mirrors and cameras. I know it's hard at times to see the truth of how you are living and who you really are but isn't it worse to go through the motions day to day? It's okay to be human and we get to begin again, however we want to, as our best, knowing that we're always at choice over and over again. Doing our best to love and lead as our best is enough, every time. And our best just keeps getting better.

WHAT RUNS YOU?

Suffering isn't me and it isn't you. I gave up suffering and everything changed. My broken heart began to heal. I learned how to have a new relationship with pain that allowed me to have the experience of life I had been longing for, because I now had a new relationship with myself, love, and possibility. Suffering is really just a longing for more life and more love. But it shuts life out. It's always an option but it comes with high stakes and so much to lose. We fight what is unhealed in our hearts and wish it away. Pain only gets louder and spreads, like cancer, until it's healed. Have you ever heard the phrase, "If you don't heal what hurts you, you will bleed on those who didn't cut you"? We have all been bleeding hearts with heartbreak. We're not alone. We're in this together. You are not the only one. Hear this, you have never been broken. It's your heart that is broken. And that beautiful and precious broken heart of yours can heal. Avoiding your broken heart and choosing to suffer instead is the opposite of courage. What if, now that you are reading these words, suffering becomes a choice you make? Self-protection and sacrifice are heavy. You decided the world can't handle you and you keep proving yourself right. It's nonsense! It's for sure easier to wish the world would slow down, change, or take care of us. Your past and your pain can go in peace, and will, if you will allow yourself to live with and lead in courage, through your struggle, instead of suffering, so you can heal.

Surrendering into possibility even in the face of the pain keeps the door open—to more life, more love, more miracles. It's a decision. Suffering or possibility. I choose possibility over and over again and because of that I'm living the life of my dreams. You can have that too when you step into your best and let that be enough. Your next level of your best can allow the unraveling of survival and your ego to make room for who you are and who you are becoming. I used to wake up every day with dread. I used to tell people I was half alive. My nervous system didn't begin to calm down until I turned forty. That only happened because I learned to see the world through my own eyes instead of through the lens of other people's perceptions and my unhealed emotional wounds. Give up suffering so that you can reinvent yourself. Suffering has to die if you want to be free.

It's easy to lead and live inspired when everything is going well or when we are flying high and in fresh love with life. When we are in hell that's when it matters the most to commit to being our best. Letting the world see you own who you are, as you allow yourself to be with and live your truth, is the ultimate in letting your freak flag fly. For so many years I'd cross my fingers in hopes that shit would work out, while I wanted to kill myself. The hard truth is that back then, I wasn't as committed as I thought I was to the life I wanted. Victim thinking and victim consciousness had me hypnotized into believing my pain, and then I would want to give up and quit because I truly didn't think I was capable. I was frozen in defeat. Feeling defeated is a downward spiral. It's the one trigger that can and does really bring us all down. Instead, get loud about wanting to quit, admit it but don't quit. Instead feel your way through your fear and resistance to prove to yourself that you can get to the other side. It's okay to *want* to quit, but don't when it comes to your dreams. Let them watch. You let them watch you suffer. Why not let them watch you break through any and all limitations as you finally hold up your white flag of hope for the world to see? Let's get real and talk about the possibility of coming through for you, for your life, instead of letting your dream of having a healthy and healed relationship with your life get further and further away.

Proceed as the best of you, loud, and proud. We all have moments where it absolutely feels like we are being beaten up and beaten down and being set up to fail. We feel alone and unsupported until we *show up for ourselves.* We all fight the *huge* self-doubt that is there whispering in our ear, flirting with us and taunting us to throw in the towel on hoping for more and better. You may think you are destined to suffer. I've been there. I have felt like a fraud in my life and I didn't get that was only because I was being so careless, irresponsible, disconnected and uncommitted to looking in the mirror and facing who I really am underneath the facade. It's time to end the war with ourselves and get out of survival mode.

It's time to *feel*. Emotions: why are they so scary? I see and meet people daily who are afraid to feel. I see people bottling up what is real for them and eventually either they shut down in complete depression and become walking zombie people, a shadow of their really phenomenal selves, or they become a tsunami of emotion that is going to take out anything and anyone in its path. The reason that we've got to talk about emotion in a book about coming back to life, is because it's the lack of emoting, aka moving through our emotions, that has us dying inside. This fear of feeling is why we blame the world (external factors) for our own refusal to step up and live.

I'm no scientist, psychiatrist, or researcher, so please excuse the generalizations that are about to follow. This book is, simply, my education and experience. It's what has and hasn't worked to support me, my clients and audiences, in genuinely feeling how we want to feel. First, your feelings about what is happening or about what happened are not the same as how you are feeling deep down. We're about to go into how to know the difference. This is where you are about to begin the process of becoming your own healer. Feelings can look like stories, thoughts, or beliefs. Feelings start with a thought about what is happening. For example, I can have a thought that anxiety is perpetually running through my veins and ruining my life. Then the feelings I'm having about my situation escalate. I feel hopeless, I can't do anything to change this, I just have to manage, I just have to get by, and there is no end in sight. When we follow our feelings about what is happening we're in big trouble and life is painful because we're stuck in our heads. It's important to start with what we're feeling in our minds so that we can get to the root of how we're feeling emotionally. Feelings start in our minds. Then we can connect to how we're feeling emotionally in our hearts and in our bodies; then life can feel spiritually free. Freedom is a spiritual feeling and experience but we can't arrive there in our heads, refusing to connect to our emotions that live in our bodies. Take what you want for you and leave the rest. Almost four decades of carrying the weight of overwhelming guilt, shame and emotional pain was enough for me. I believe that I survived so that I can share what I have learned with you. So, here goes.

Let's talk about our emotions that live underneath our feelings about what's happening outside of us. Notice, I'm not saying to you "Let's talk about our feelings." I'm saying let's feel our feelings by using our awareness to connect to our bodies. This is the head to heart connection that is the key to a new lease on life. We can't think our way into feeling better. Feelings begin with the story that we tell ourselves about what "happened." That's important but next it's time to look at and connect to how we actually feel, emotionally, underneath the story. The stuck emotion underneath the story is the infection you carry that needs to be felt all the way through, and can, come out and heal. The feelings we live about the story often keeps us in the story. I'll give you an example. I've already shared some about my childhood sexual abuse.

It mostly happened in a bed. So, when I grew up and had lovers that wanted to have sex in the middle of the night, for a long time I felt re-traumatized and like a wreck when I would wake up to a partner initiating sex. The story that I had about what I thought was happening to me, I'm not safe, I'm being taken advantage of, etc., masked the emotion (what I needed to feel) that I just would not let myself feel—*ANGER*. See how this works? We have to get the emotion out in a way that isn't lashing out, it's just release in a healthy way. If I only stayed focused on feeling like I was being taken advantage of, used, dirty, and violated, then the stuck emotions underneath my "feelings" of fear, grief, and anger had nowhere to go. When my grandmother died the shock had me frozen, feeling confusion and betrayal. I swallowed the emotions of fear, grief and anger with my tears, buried them deep, and I got very stuck. All that was needed was emotional release but I didn't know that for most of my life so I stayed stuck in painful patterns. When we only get real about what we're feeling it's not enough to break the pattern.

When my aunt said, "He doesn't love you for your body," I don't know what she meant but I can tell you what I made that mean about me. *That*, right there, was another heartbreak and another betrayal with a woman. See how the patterns keep picking up the pace and repeat? I shut my heart and my emotion of "anger" down, and stopped being willing to fully risk being all of me, and loving as much as I am capable of, for too many years. In one moment we shut down; but in one moment we can also come back to life if we will feel all the way through our stuck emotions.

I am a lover. If I love you, you are going to be loved hard, deep, and fast, and I don't mean romantically. And if I meet you, I will fall in love with you, unapologetically, because you are gorgeous. I want to live and love fiercely. Anything else feels terrible to me. But that day, with my grandmother, then again that day on that car ride, I decided that I wasn't lovable and I would have to make up for it. I decided that

I would have to live in spite of. Meanwhile, my heart shut down more and more because I couldn't be with my stuck emotions that I needed to feel, yet. Feeling the fear, grief, and anger in a healthy way would have allowed me to eventually feel joy and excitement. We can't ignore the darker emotions and get to feel the good stuff. It's all or nothing. It's this simple. Not easy, but simple.

STEP 1: What am I feeling about what is happening?

STEP 2: What is my body needing to feel underneath that story?

STEP 3: What emotion (fear, anger, grief, excitement, joy) wants to be and needs to be released now?

The only thing that will help when you are in any sort of emotional pain is feeling your way through your emotions. Say it out loud, "It is safe to feel my emotions. They can't hurt me." And please know it was never other people's emotions that hurt you either, it was their inability to feel and release their emotions in a healthy and safe way that was the problem. Having feelings isn't helping. Feeling your emotions is the path to freedom and the life that you want. I promise.

Here's the secret sauce magic formula to feeling extraordinary:

1. FEELINGS. Know the difference between what you are feeling and what emotion you need to feel.

2. FEEL. Feel the emotion all the way, and in a way that doesn't harm you or anyone else.

3. FREEDOM. Remember that you are at choice. Powerfully choose and decide what takes care of you now, who you are going to be now, know what you are needing and wanting, and give it to yourself.

It's brave to know and understand what you are feeling. It's even braver to actually feel your way through the emotions underneath those feelings until you come out the other side. That's vulnerability. That's what creates emotional intimacy. And intimacy means your soul is free and clear and able to be connected to your best self and to other people without your survival personality and your unhealed past getting in the way. Now, let's go deeper into emotions.

Think of your emotions like what a baby feels. Babies have zero story or feelings going on about the world and what the happenings of the world mean about them. The story we tell ourselves about what is happening and what that means about us is what hurts. Babies feel their senses, that's it. They cry when they need to, laugh when they need to, yell when they need to. They have a healthy relationship with fear, and they are happy. Again, let's make this simple. The practice of emotional healing only looks at five emotions. That's it. Underneath the oceans of feelings that we can have about what's happening inside us because of what's happening around us, there are only five emotions to look for that are the culprits of every single upset that ever was.

FEAR

ANGER

GRIEF

JOY

EXCITEMENT

We can feel all of this at once or a mix all at once. A baby can move through these emotions in seconds, *we can, too.* We just learned not to because it wasn't accepted or safe or received well in our families growing up. The big thing here is that there are no good or bad emotions. There are no positive or negative emotions. There are darker emotions, such as fear, anger, and grief, and lighter emotions, such as excitement and joy. If you won't feel the dark you don't get to feel the light. They all matter. None of these emotions can hurt you or anyone else. It's the refusal to feel them *all* fully that creates the madness that goes on inside. There are just five emotions and if you won't feel your way through every single one of them whenever they need you to feel them, you don't get to feel free. Emotions are always neutral. We've been trying to avoid the world's reactions to our emotions and what's now on the table for you is to give that old paradigm up and model freely feeling, from your heart, so that others can see that it's safe for them to feel, too.

Fear

Fear is just an emotional message that you are uncertain about an unknown. You are in uncharted waters. You don't know what to do. You don't know what someone else is going to do. You don't know whether or not you can do what needs to be done. Fear says, *I don't know if I can do this. I don't know if I can handle this.* But you always have what you need—especially if you are emotionally clear. Panic isn't fear. Anxiety isn't fear. Frozen isn't fear. Panic, anxiety, and frozen are all ways we learned to cope with and avoid the perceived pain of feeling our way through fear. There was a time when you didn't question yourself or life because of an unknown. You trusted yourself, how you were feeling, let yourself feel, and knew that your needs would be met and that it was safe to be authentically who you really were. Many of us learned fear was "wrong or bad" very, very young. The same is true for the four following emotions. It was never the emotion. It was the reaction that we got to the emotion that stalled us out and stopped us in our tracks and then the emotion got stuck in our bodies and had nowhere to go. What I'm saying is, fear isn't bad or wrong; it's natural, human, and not going anywhere, so we might as well make friends with it and use it to our advantage when we find ourselves feeling and needing to feel our way through real fear that deserves to be acknowledged, respected, and moved through. So how do you move through fear in a safe, non-threatening, healthy way? Here are some ideas: Breathe. Meditate. Swim, shower, or take a bath and wash it all away. Write: Give your fears a voice so that you can take your power back. Make a list of your greatest accomplishments and remember who you really are. Walk: put one foot in front of the other, proving to yourself that you can go farther than you think you can. Light a candle and let it represent your life and your light. Take it in. It's so beautiful. You are so beautiful.

Anger

Anger is an emotional message that you are passionate about something. It's an emotion that is demanding that you finally take a stand for your right to be here taking up space in the world as the leader you were born to be. Anger says, I matter. My life matters. Anger never hurt anyone. It's not violence. It's not mean. It's not mad. All that is fighting with ghosts and external factors. The people who were violent, mean, and taking that out on you or those you loved, didn't know what to do with or about their anger. And that isn't their fault. No one taught them. They didn't know how. They thought love meant taking their pain out on those they cared about. And you are here to learn, experience and model a new way. Anger is passion. It's an emotion that is demanding that you finally take a stand for your right to be here taking up space in the world as the leader you were born to be. So how do you move through anger in a safe, non-threatening, healthy way? Here are some ideas: Scream, from the diaphragm, not your throat. Let your primal voice be heard far and wide. Write. Get it all out, and give your anger a voice so that it's not stuck inside of you anymore. Move your body, listen to music, breathe, meditate, rip up an old phone book, get a punching bag, go to a thrift shop and get dishes and break them. The point is get it out, not at anybody, not at yourself—*just out.* All the way out.

Grief

Grief is an emotional message that you are letting go of something that you loved very much. Grief is what keeps our hearts open. Grief is the full expression of the sadness that could shut our hearts down if we're not careful. Grief doesn't mean we're weak or a victim. It means we cared with all of our hearts. It shows us that life has changed and won't ever go back to how it was before. When we grieve we make room for miracles, possibility, and more love. The sadness is okay. So how do you move through grief in a safe, non-threatening, healthy way? Here are some ideas. Cry until it gets gentler, and it will. You have got to get it out. Let the tears flow, then find a way to practice self-care in a gentle way. Write love letters and goodbye letters, even to those who have passed, or to people, places, and things that you aren't willing or ready to face. Face them now on paper and let yourself grieve how much you loved, how much you cared, and how much you gave. Do not let grief shut your heart down. You will feel so much lighter and as you grieve you make room for excitement, joy and what's to come.

Excitement

Excitement is an emotional message that you have an opportunity to pursue and experience something you love. Excitement means that you are looking forward to your life in the moment you are in, knowing even better is on the way. Being excited means that you know who you are, you are fully alive, and you are living how you want to be living. Excitement is natural. Excitement is healthy. Excitement is allowed. Watch out for the fear that if you get too excited something could go wrong or that the other shoe could drop. If you, like me, were sexually abused or have experienced trauma with another person of any kind, know that person wasn't excited by you, or excited to hurt you, even if it looked like that. They were also abused or traumatized, and they didn't know how to be with their emotions. They were running, and powerless, and in a very dark hell. They were attracted to your light but they didn't extinguish it. You are still bright and burning your beautiful light and get to be excited about what that light that is in you shows you about what life can offer you now. So how do you move through excitement in a safe, non-threatening, healthy way? Here are some ideas: Let yourself have it. Get present to the beauty that is in you and all around you, always. Write about the most exciting parts of your day before you go to sleep. Keep an excitement journal where you let yourself dream about what you want, what you desire, what you are creating, and what you are most passionate about. Take time to be in nature and feel the power of life, and the power of your life. Get still. Practice silence—let yourself connect to the best of you. Practice being present in the moment without fear of the future or focus on the past. Being excited about right here, right now, truly is all that there is.

Joy

Joy is the emotional message that you are fully in love with you and your life, exactly as it is, in the moment you are in, and you are genuinely unlimited and beautifully authentic. Joy is your birthright.

It means that you feel safe within yourself, your nervous system is relaxed, you are peacefully knowing that life is exactly as it should be, and that you deserve to experience the best that life has to offer you. Joy isn't because of circumstances. Joy isn't toxic positivity. It's an emotion that radiates from within you out into the world because you've removed all blocks to love and receiving. So how do you move through joy in a safe, non-threatening, healthy way? Here are some ideas: Trust it! Nothing bad is going to happen because you let yourself feel joy. Let yourself cry! Tears don't only come in the color of grief. Tears of joy are the most pure and beautiful tears of all and tears of grief become tears of joy when you do your deepest work and live into and practice emotional healing in all moments.

TIME TO FEEL

Feelings are different than *feeling*. Feeling is the answer. Feeling takes you up and out of the experience of life that you are having and into a new experience. Feelings can keep you down. The goal is always to get to an experience of life that feels good no matter the situation. And it's possible. Remember, when you are hurting an emotion is stuck inside you. Be brave enough to let it out. At first, there may be a flood because these emotions have been backlogged. Don't let that scare you. There is an end to the pain. There is a light at the end of the tunnel. There is a new beginning of emotional healing on the way. Once you get through the backlog you just have to keep up with feeling each emotion, every one, every time it's needing you to feel it. You get to feel free and stay free by becoming emotionally clear. We feel our best when we're emotionally clear. We lead better and love better when we're emotionally clear. Many people want to do anything but emote, but that's the permanent ticket out of emotional hell. The key to emoting in a way that will free you up is to first and foremost, understand that emoting, moving through emotions is healthy, strong, and necessary if you want to leave emotional pain in your past. Second, never ever take your emotions and upsets out on other human beings. Emoting means letting the naturally occurring emotions of fear, anger, grief, excitement, and joy out because they need to come out. Please note that situations do not cause emotions. The emotions are stuck and when they bubble up to the surface, know these truths: First, they can't hurt you. Second, they need to come out. Where so many are innocently mistaken is when they think that a person or situation caused their emotion. The emotions are in you until you feel your way through them. People and life will show you where you have emotional wounds that are ready to heal. Consider that it will be someone or something else "triggering you" until the wound is healed because you did the work to emotionally release. Therefore, if the particular situation or individual in front of you wasn't the emotional trigger, it would be someone or something else. I believe that the situation or person that you are upset about brought about an opportunity for your soul's healing. Taking our emotions out on people and lashing out is so not the solution and will keep you spinning your wheels.

Feelings are thoughts about what happened, and they are learned. For example, we aren't born knowing that we can be rejected, betrayed, jealous, abandoned, wounded, depressed, or anxious. We learn these ways of being with our upset and can easily slip into believing that the external factor was the cause. Avoiding your emotions and being stuck in your head creates a turbulent undercurrent in our lives. In any "upset" situation there is an emotion to move through, and if you don't do so you block joy.

It's time to get out of the hamster wheel and move through those stuck emotions. Make sense? If not, that's okay. Just start to consider what I'm suggesting here. I know that my words basically go against everything we've ever been taught. But are you starting to see the light? We want to make our emotions wrong but they aren't wrong, they are real, beautiful even. Too often we want to take them out on people, and by the way, the wrong people. We fight with our pasts and with the ghosts of our pasts and ruin our right now. It doesn't have to been this way. Cry when you need to cry. Scream if you need to scream. Shake if you need to shake. Or you won't ever be able to freely laugh when you want to laugh and sing when you want to sing. Let's step into an emotionally orgasmic life where we are fully expressed and free. Idealistic, sure. Possible, I choose to believe. Will you join me?

I want to acknowledge the growth available to all of us. Stuck emotions, like the truth, need to be acknowledged. Have you ever noticed that you get further with people and have more success in relationships when you acknowledge the truth? Our emotions are craving acknowledgment and often we are in an acknowledgment drought when it comes to the truth about how we feel. Acknowledgment means we're no longer willing to look the other way. We get to face the emotional music, and it leads to so much goodness when we do.

Happiness is a willingness and understanding that we can be fully feeling all five emotions—fear, anger, grief, joy, excitement—all at the same time, or whenever they show up. I can be happy when I am connected to my emotional body and not threatened by it. My emotional guidance system is magnificent and shows me how aligned I am living as my real self. For me, life is a constant experience of moving through fear while I passionately stand for myself and others, while I let go and grieve what was, making room for more, while I let myself be excited about life as it is now and as I know it will be, while I bask in the joy and deliciousness of being alive. I want you to have your version of all of this, so please, keep reading. Happiness isn't circumstantial. Just like emotional pain, happiness doesn't happen to us or come from outside of us. Watch out for guilty pleasures or escapes that feel good in a moment but are really just avoidance to feeling your emotions all the way through.

The stories and feelings we live that break our hearts show up as patterns that we repeat later in life. Your pain will continue and carry on, getting heavier, until you let yourself move through your stuck emotions. I promise. This is not a threat, it's a real promise. Life is just life. The moments and events that we have all been through or are going through now are neutral. They mean nothing. It's like the little mermaid Ariel brushing her hair with a fork. So what? The fork means nothing, she has zero story or feelings about the fork and creatively decides to brush her hair with it and she lets herself feel excitement and joy unapologetically. The events and moments of our lives are a lot like that fork. They mean nothing until we decide to make up a long, drawn-out story about "it," whatever "it" was. We focus on the events instead of on the emotion underneath the events. That's how patterns start and continue. If we would just face and feel our emotions, all the way, we could put the fork in the story and the pattern and be complete with that part of our heartbreak.

Emotions are natural, normal, and again, neutral. They are real and as old as when humanity was born. Again, I'm not a scientist, so I don't claim to be an expert here or know the scientific facts about emotion, but please allow me to share what I've seen in my clients, friends, family members, and in myself. First of all, if you won't *feel,* you cannot be *free.* You are the only source of your freedom. Consider that any place you may be feeling trapped is *not* because of your circumstances, it's because you have a stuck emotion that you will not *feel* your way through because of your feelings about what's happening. Remember, feeling your emotions is not the same as having a feeling. For example, having a feeling of defeat and sourcing from that place of feeling defeated can come with collateral damage. If we take the feeling deeper we can get to the emotion or emotions underneath and feel or emote all the way until we are emotionally clear.

Full disclosure: At first when you relax into your emotions, face and feel them, it may feel like you will never be able to stop crying. As you begin feeling the emotions all the way through, the floodgates do open and the dam will burst because it needed to. Thing is, if you won't feel, the weight of carrying your stuck emotion and all that's stuck behind that dam will weigh you down with every breath you take. And it can make you sick. You can let out your stuck emotions now and start leading your life from where you are. You don't have to wait until external factors change to begin to powerfully lead your life. Stop waiting for life to change before you start to live and feel. Once you recognize you have stuck emotions that you are more ready to release than you may believe, hire a professional to support you with this part. It's the biggest piece to coming back to life, and support and professional help is a strong recommendation to assist you in fully healing pain, trauma, and heartbreak. The most courageous thing you can do for yourself is allowing your stuck emotions to surface and be released, but have support. Support makes opening up Pandora's Box less scary. You may think it's not worth it or it would make it even more painful to open up this box but resistance is futile because what's in Pandora's Box is running and potentially even ruining your life already. What's in the way of you living and experiencing life the way you've longed for is all that is in there. And you are stronger and way more powerful than anything in that box.

The weight of not emoting is killing off your soul, one stuck and unshed tear at a time. It doesn't have to be this way. There are only two options when it comes to emotions. The first is to feel to heal, so that you can release in a healthy way. Be with that heavy emotion, let it go all the way, and let it out. Ugly cry. It just might save your life. The key is to own your emotions responsibly. This means not taking your emotions out on each other. One more time: please, never take your emotions out on other people. Yes, even if you think they deserve it. Haven't we all already been hurt enough? Haven't we all been through enough? What's the benefit of emotionally moving through everything that you absolutely do not want to feel, you ask? It's you getting in charge of being your own source of freedom. Do you want to feel free in your life as the rule, not the exception? It's your choice. You get to choose how you will live. Path one gets you free. Embrace the magnitude of who you are by feeling through your emotions and heartbreak.

Path two, welcome to hell and a heaviness to the point where you might not even feel like you can breathe or like it's worth it to keep living. Path two is you fighting through your life and shutting down your heart and dimming your brilliantly bright spirit. Path two is suffering. It's the self-inflicted suffocation of your soul. Give yourself permission to let you out, including your emotions (which are your humanity), or you will inevitably suffer. This is me talking to your soul. There is a way of healing that you might not know about or

believe is possible for you—that way is emotional healing. I'm here
to tell you that you are made of emotion, beauty, and that your voice
matters. Your body holds all three of these gifts that only you can give
to yourself and the world. You can only give the world as much of you
as you are willing to face. The healing doesn't hurt you; it's refusing
to heal that is hurting you.

What would it be like to wake up every day and look in the mirror and say, "Good morning, you sexy, beautiful, messy, badass, rock
star!"? To tell yourself, "Let's feel our way through this day. Let's slay
this day, being as much of you as you can possibly be. Get it, in all
of your glory"? Maybe you think this sounds absurd. Or maybe you
think this sounds glorious. Either way, what I know to be true is
that if you keep going the way you are going, when it comes to your
triggers, you'll end up at the same heartbreak and dead stop that you
hit, over and over again.

Have you ever felt like a caged animal? Me too. It's *not* your circumstances. It's holding back your voice, your truth, and not letting
yourself feel. I am literally screaming from the mountaintops: let
yourself out! Let your emotions out. Or don't and climb the walls day
after day only to fall back to the ground again, wishing and hoping
there was a way out. There is—it's you.

We won't feel because our hearts broke. I've never met a person
who did not have a broken heart. Notice that I am not saying that I've
never met a person who at one time did not have a broken heart. *I've
never met a person whose heart was not still broken.* Our hearts break
and we think that we are broken. No, your *heart* is broken, now. I can
almost guarantee it. That's because you are *alive* and human and here.
Our hearts can be broken and stay open at the same time. That's where
the magic happens. We don't know how to keep our broken hearts

open so that we can keep living and loving. We all have that first heartbreak and then we think that the solution is to self-protect as we shut our broken hearts down, because we decided at the moment our heart broke that it's not safe to feel or love. Then we live in hell refusing to fully express ourselves. Full expression means fully feeling, fully living, fully talking, and fully loving as much of you as you can be. It's your right to live free, inspired, and fully expressed—which is all really just the same thing.

REFLECTIONS

The mirror has been my number one enemy. It won't and can't lie. It's left me leveled and on my knees both metaphorically and literally. And it's given me my life by showing me what I didn't even know that I needed to see. I avoided mirrors for decades not wanting to see the truth about who I was, who I'd been, but even more, the lies I was living. Every lie weighed more than I ever will and carried a heaviness that is immeasurable. The weight on my shoulders that constricted my chest and made it hard to sleep, or breathe, or eat, or feel, or live, came from the lies I told myself about my worth, my flaws, my perceived wretchedness, how not capable and unlovable I believed I was; it goes on and on. I thought this was normal and told myself these lies every day beginning at just four years old. I no longer offer up lies about myself that hurt me as a prayer to the world. Prayers get answered. Instead of being committed to proving myself right about my worst fears about myself, now I chase possibility and more life.

Untruths only hurt us and keep us separate from our highest selves and separate from everyone we meet. The mirror has been the forever enemy of many. But it's also our savior because it shows me, me, and it shows you, you. As I look into my own eyes, the mirror can't and won't lie. It won't whisper what I want to hear in my ear. The mirror represents how I'm living and what I believe, and it shows me I'm still here, in this body, and in this life. And it shows me how and what I need to feel. We're all deserving, capable, and precious with so much abundance available. Any belief that hurts can be transformed. Any stuck emotion can be expressed. We can find the beliefs that serve us and the ones that hurt us when we look in the mirror. Today as I glance into the window of my soul I like what I see. If I can break up with self-loathing for good, so can you.

MIRROR WORK

My coach gave me the assignment to look at myself in the mirror naked until I loved what I saw. I am a very committed student and I always do my homework. But this assignment was terrifying. The night I took it on was cold and who knows how many boxes of tissues I went through. At the time, I lived in a little carriage house with a leaky ceiling with my three-year-old. It was windy. Petrified, I holed up in my room, got out a mirror, got naked, and entered into one of the greatest battles of my life with myself. In a matter of hours, I went from believing that there was no way to win that battle of self-hatred and shame, to full-on surrender into healing, release, and hope. Looking back, the fight was only about whether or not I was *willing to let go* of the weight of self-doubt and self-loathing. Everything at the time was my body's fault. I blamed my innocent body for everything that had ever gone wrong in my life: being overlooked, bullied, abused, cheated on, being broke, being alone, being left out, being misunderstood. And this list was just the beginning. The physical, emotional, and spiritual weight was really there, knocking the wind out of me, along with my heartbreak, as I stared into myself. A person I hated. A person I was committed to hating and beating down. And then it occurred to me: *No wonder I feel like the world is beating me down day after day and like the hits just keep coming. I am awful to myself. Oh my God, I am awful to myself.* Then my thoughts began to race as I thought about my innocent daughter sleeping peacefully in the next room. I had to change this energy, this dark force of misery that was killing my spirit and taking me away from her. And then I heard my own voice, so soft, barely recognizable, saying out loud, "If I won't face this weight and heartbreak, how will I ever be able to release?" Somehow, I knew that my inherited pain patterns would repeat and get passed on to my gorgeous baby girl unless I had the courage to heal my broken heart. I knew enough to know that my broken heart at sixteen felt the same at twenty-seven when I divorced my first husband. What if I didn't have to manage my way through life with a broken heart? What if I was still in there, in that body, beneath all of that pain?

That was the day that I began to be the hero that came to my own rescue. It was a lie that I was so bad that I only deserved to be living in hell. It was fake for me to live like I was less than. It was time to change the course of my life forever, for the better, and I did. Confession time. That day, I went from wanting to die, from years of lying awake in bed every night fantasizing about taking a knife and cutting the literal and metaphorical fat out of me and ending my life, to finally beginning to live. I committed to life. I took Sharpie markers and wrote out my thoughts about myself and my worth all over my body. I faced them. I read the words. Words like ugly, fat, disgusting, stupid, worthless, gross, idiot. I saw them. Until I saw myself and it didn't hurt anymore. This may sound counterintuitive, but I needed to see on my own skin what I was believing about myself and saying to myself because those words represented a reality that was not healthy. Once I saw the words, I could finally see that they were just words, not facts about me. One by one, each word lost its power and no longer felt like a part of my identity. I began to create a blank canvas and began to choose who I wanted to be and how I wanted to see myself.

Commitment to the life you want includes being willing to look in the mirror. Honesty is healing medicine. We can only prove ourselves right about what we say and believe about ourselves. What you say *is true for you.* Once your story and beliefs change, they won't come out of your mouth ever again. Let's talk about commitment. Such a big word. Such a strong word. Such a not-taken-seriously-enough word. If you want to be free, *commit to your internal guidance system, become your own healer, and follow your emotions to joy.* Commitment to life is possible in the face of anything and requires care and attention. What would happen if you committed courageously to being who it took to have the life you want? If you took on being the person it took to live your life your way, what about your commitment to yourself would have to change?

ON SELF-RESPONSIBILITY

The mission is healing. The cure is always self-responsibility. It's not your fault, wherever you find yourself. Whatever happened that broke your heart, happened. It's over. You made it. Now your only job is to live free, fully expressed, and healed, regardless of what you have been through. The darkness is real and so is the light.

The light in you can and will guide you home, back to the you that you really are. To the highest version of you that has all of your answers. There isn't a wrong way or a right way to live your life; there is only what works for you.

Your life is waiting for you to lean in. Waiting for you to relax. Waiting for you to lead in the unique and gentle way that has you going to bed at night certain of who you were that day, and confident about who you will be—that glorious rock star you really are—when you wake up in the morning.

When was the last time you looked into your own eyes and loved what you saw? When was the last time that you experienced your greatness? It starts by taking on willingness. Willingness to feel. Willingness to show your heart and soul to the world. Willingness to fall in love with every life in front of you starting with your own. Willingness to see yourself and others as innocent and doing their best as they desperately try to heal what seems impossible to heal.

You can learn how to *be willing to be willing*. And to understand what it means to be clear, present, and dangerous because you have officially become unapologetically whole. Your relationship with your life is your job. Your upsets are never, ever, anyone else's fault. They aren't your fault either but it's up to you to change your experience of stress and suffering. It's up to you to move the energy that feels off. To access possibilities in even the darkest and most difficult times. To be your best even when it seems like it's not worth it. It's always worth it. It's always better to give more and be more and love more because when you do you make the world a better place.

Your relationships are also up to you to heal, repair, and reinvent, and they are also a mirror giving you more access to you. They give you access to where your next healing opportunity lies. You get to see how far you've come and what is next to clear out of your way on your path through the eyes of others and because of all of your relationships. The words you hear and the way you see the world through all of your relationships shows you your relationship with yourself and with your life, always. The moments that take your breath away and the moments that knock the wind out of you are all so important. They all give you access to more life and remind you that you are still here.

It's easy to live safe, small, and in self-protection mode but it costs so much. It's harder to break through survival mode and to heal your survival personality that doesn't trust that there is life beyond self-protection. But life outside of safety and self-protection is where the healing happens. It's where magic and miracles exist. You think people hurt you. You think people don't see or hear or value you. They are where they are with their relationship with themselves, their past, and with their lives. They show you who you've been and offer you the gift of the chance to rise to the occasion of being your best self. Even if they are slimy, mean, shut down, or seemingly not worth it, you get to heal and grow and live into the version of you that you've always wanted to be. So that you can live the life you've been dying to live. It's not happening to you or for you. It's just life. Now, who will you be?

When you are willing to be responsible for your reality, your experience, your choices, and your impact, nothing can harm you, ever again.

When you refuse to adapt down into that lesser, heartbroken, lashing-out version of you and instead choose to be, give, and show love to yourself and every life in front of you, you can know that you have become the exact medicine that humanity and our planet so desperately needs right now. We are each responsible for our impact, our healing, and how we feel about our lives. Maybe you've forgotten how to love your life, or how to be your best. But know that you are a healer, leader, teacher, and an inspiration. We need you, at your best.

Journal EXERCISE

- What was your first heartbreak? How old were you?
  What happened?

- Where do you dim yourself down?

- Where are you faking it in your life?

- What is your relationship now with fear?

- What is your relationship now with anger?

- What is your relationship now with grief?

- What is your relationship now with excitement?

- What is your relationship now with joy?

- MIRROR WORK: Spend at least ten minutes (set a timer)
  looking at and taking yourself in. Journal your truths,
  thoughts, realizations, and takeaways.

Chapter Three

THE PAIN

No matter what your fears or the ultimate reality of you stepping into your life as a free bird would entail, the life you long for is waiting for you.

The wind is touching me without my permission. I don't want to feel my body, it hurts too much. The wind, blowing me kisses and stroking my hair, makes me want to stick needles in my eyes. I'm in a convertible and I'm *hot.* It's summer. It's *Florida.* My body confuses me. I don't trust it. He tells me if I'm so hot I should take my shirt off. This isn't making me feel safe. We're alone. We are waiting for them. I'm twelve maybe? Feeling fat. Feeling hot. Not wanting to feel the wind. Not wanting to feel the sweat. Not wanting to feel his words soaking into my skin like suntan lotion. I want to disappear so I don't have to face or feel my "right now." I feel dirty. I feel disgusted. But I won't let myself go there. It would hurt too much and make things worse if I yelled and screamed or cried or ran away. Instead, I decide that I must be disgusting. I eat the pain. I already know how to cover up how I really feel what I really need, what I really want. The possibility of me being able to get my needs met is so foreign at twelve years old that it doesn't occur to me that my emotions are valid and that what's happening is inappropriate. I am living in a toxic environment that is harmful to me and I think to myself, *this is just how it is, how it's going to be,* and I lean on what I've learned which is to adapt, adjust, and shut down my voice and my truth.

⸎

We take on the pain. We own the pain. We cover up our souls with our pain. We cover up our bodies with our pain. We won't let ourselves be seen as raw and vulnerable. A coach once said to me that raw wasn't an attractive word. I don't care. Raw is fresh, and real, and juicy, and as God intended. Many people only eat raw food. It's gorgeous and nutritious and real. What would it be like to take down the self-structured and oh-so-carefully created barricades covering up who we are? As Elsa sings in *Frozen,* "Don't let them in, don't let them see . . ." Why? What's the benefit of this insane way of living? Together but alone in your truth. Surrounded by hundreds, thousands, millions, and billions of people, but alone with the truth of who you are. I cannot think of any benefits to this. I can only see more suffering and more emotional pain. We wrap ourselves up in essentially a straitjacket of trapped fear, and it's so heavy.

Now I'm going to tell you the story of the first time that I knew, I knew it, like you know when it's raining because it pricks at your skin and makes your hair wet and gets in your shoes. I knew the world couldn't handle my pain and that I wasn't supposed to get too excited about life. And yes, we have to go there. We have to. If you won't that's okay but then the straitjacket just gets tighter. The pain piles on. You'll have a hard time breathing. You'll have a hard time loving. You'll have a hard time hearing your soul screaming at you to take off the jacket. It's easy to not even notice that we are getting heavier and less alive because we lost our ability to be honest about our emotions and our pain.

THE BATHING SUIT

I'm out in the sun getting ready to swim. I don't think I'm smart at twelve. I don't think I'm good at anything except for reading and swimming. I'm not good at friends, school, or music, even though I want to be good at all of these things. My parents send me to summer camp every year now. I get to swim and at night I get to read. At camp I can escape from the cold war and the battles in my house. I get to be a stranger for a week or two anyway. My favorite part of camp is swimming. Swimming is where I can float. It's the only time that I actually want to be in and feel my body. I feel my strength in the water. I trust myself in the water. I want to be in the water on this particular day, even though it means wearing a bathing suit.

Another thing that I love about summer camp is that I don't have to strategize or analyze or try to predict what is coming, what I need to protect myself and my family from, or what could go wrong. I have blind faith and trust and I feel safe here. I get two weeks outside, in the water, climbing, camping, getting messy, getting away. It's magical. In the morning we are supposed to layer up with bathing suits under our clothes so when it's time to swim we're ready to go. I've always been impatient; I may be the most impatient person I know. On this particular day I don't want to take the time required to get my bathing suit all the way on because it's way too tight. I can't breathe in it. So I don't put it on all the way. I leave my arms out and let the bathing suit sit at my waist squeezing me like a tourniquet. The fun begins, the day goes on, and I forget I'm not fully covered when it's time to swim. Along with the other kids who were ripping off layers and taking off full throttle into the water, I take off my shirt and then am immediately horrified to discover that I am topless.

Everyone is looking at me. I am so embarrassed. This may go down in history as my most embarrassing moment of all time. I have to think fast. There was a boy nearby who I decided to pin this on. I start to cry, hard, carrying incredible shame. The camp counselors know I'm full of it. No one is getting in trouble. I just want to die. The pain is unbearable. The pain is too much. I can't be responsible for it. I can't face it. I have to deflect. To survive. To protect myself. To protect the world from what would happen if I really let it all out.

I was reminded not to get too excited that day. It cost too much. It was too embarrassing and shameful. Excitement was foolish, confusing, and bad. The sexual abuse that my body had already experienced felt dirty, bad, and wrong. It was also the result of excitement, wasn't it? I felt lost in my abuse. I had decided long before this day by the water that excitement meant bad things. *How could I have let myself forget that?* I decided that I wouldn't let myself get excited ever again. This was the beginning of a next level of flatlining my emotions. I doubled down on covering myself up emotionally. I buried my truth, and the pain, and began a fake way of being and living that I thought was safer. I began to act instead of live. Acting the part was easier, or so I thought. But the *real* me just got buried deeper and deeper into nothingness and slowly I forgot and disconnected from who I really was. Life became an act and I was not nearly as good of an actress as I thought that I was. It hurts to live all covered up. What I didn't know was that I was still there underneath the covers of protection that I wore like a badge of honor. The pain, yet another layer of protection, and the way out of it came later, much later.

What if we all want the same thing? We want to be seen, loved, safe, heard, supported, and celebrated. But it starts with the way you are loving, listening to, seeing, supporting and celebrating your pain. In my experience there will never be the right set of circumstances for you to get vulnerable and safe enough to be who you really are. We got helpless and stayed that way. We weren't born that way. We avoided helplessness when it came to the pain instead of knowing that we could grow up into the adult that can slay the day and any red flag or demon that shows up and surprises us. The blindsides can just be a part of our healing journey. But somewhere when we were young we got scared and stopped being willing to risk being fully seen. We stopped fully seeing ourselves. When are you going to start showing up raw and real, living as you? Your pain is not who you are. Protecting it is you coping the only way that you've ever known how. There is another way. When we cover up our souls and our pain, we're giving up our right to live.

It's a moment. And then everything changes. And you can't go back to the time before the moment that changed everything. Until now. I can help. If you will get raw with me, just until you can breathe again. And then one day being who you really are will become as natural as breathing. We decide. We know. We defend. We stand for I am too much, my pain is too much. No more!

No matter what the fears or ultimate reality of you stepping into your life as a pain-free human would entail, your life is waiting for you. The thing is, you may think there is a fee. The cost will be too great. But what if the price you are paying now to live restricted and trapped in your life is the greatest price that you could ever pay? We sit tight and sit still and play dead. You being willing to live small (while your pain feels huge) and stuck and stifled, can end. I believe that the worst crime we can commit is the crime of losing ourselves. Giving you up to fit into the world that you think that you are supposed to fit into is not only tragic, but also *totally optional.* I know it might not feel like living fully and free of the pain is an option but it is. It really is. You may have buried your ability to dream of life beyond the pain. That's what happened to me. Survival mode is most of our m.o., but we hate it. Your dreams are there, in you, at your core, and you can access them again if you decide to feel your way through your pain. It's great to live comfortably under the covers, warm, safe, and cozy on a rainy Sunday morning. But let's not live our lives covered up.

PLEASE, BREAK UP WITH BELIEVING THAT YOU ARE TRAPPED

If you want to create a new relationship and experience with your pain you will have to allow yourself to embrace the fallout of living how you are living now. I'm not going to lie. I'm pretty sure that it's going to feel uncomfortable, at first and in moments along the way. You'll have to embrace the free fall of your life now into the relationship with your pain, your body, the environment you are living in that may not be well for you, and anything else that keeps you quietly comfortable with suffering. The smoke and mirrors have to fall out of the life you are living now if you are going to feel better. I know it's scary. I know it might feel like if you start to cry you might never stop. I know it feels like if you really let the world see you getting messy and honest about your pain you might get left, dropped, rejected, or abandoned. And you might. But have you considered that you living the lie that the world can't handle you embracing and healing through your pain is costing you everything? *Everything.* This is the definition of you abandoning yourself. Another crime.

It is your right to receive. Receiving is about taking in. If you won't receive and take in all of life, including your pain, until it neutralizes, all that life offers will be put on hold. It's safe to be vulnerable. It's safe to get excited about life. It's safe to risk letting the world meet the real you. What is the alternative? If you won't go here life will get darker and it will be harder and harder to breathe. Breathe. Start breathing again, like really breathing again. Breathe into your perfectly starving-for-more belly. Right now. Why? Because it hurts too much not to feel. You don't have time to waste. Life is precious and as my first coach used to say, it's a time-limited event.

I believe that the reason why so many kids think that being an adult is going to suck is because they watch the adults in their lives avoid their pain. And they watch them go through the motions, doing what they think they should, not that happy, and certainly not free. We model living in hell day after day and our children watch us and decide their destiny. Let's set a new example. A new way of being with our pain so that our kids aren't so scared of theirs.

I will be the first to admit that going for it can often coincide with fear that the inevitable result will be a painful ending or loss. And loss may occur. We can lose the comfort of some relationships, and the parts of how we've been living that support our suffering will have to leave to make room for what is actually good and healthy for us now. Life the way it is at least makes sense somehow. The thought of the bottom falling out of how we've been living inauthentically can be paralyzing. And yet, loss makes room for more but we still want to keep what we have, the way we have it. But we can't have both. Where you are now was a great start. But if you are reading this book, you're ready to let go of how you have been living on some level. The question is, will you be brave enough to allow yourself a rebirth? All songs and dances have a beginning, middle, and end. So does your pain running your life.

For many years I had this deep fear that my pain was too much. That fear became a belief that created more evidence. And because I kept proving this trigger right, it ran through my life as an experience that would play like a favorite song on repeat, except I hated that song, and those feelings suffocated me for decades.

I'm not pretending like I'm not an intense person with big energy, big dreams, and big ideas. I want to make a big impact in this lifetime. My mission is to take people who want to get the most out of their lives along on a journey of hope and healing. I realized after decades of growth work that I don't get to have both my life's work and my pain running my life at the same time. I had to choose. You get to choose too.

When we're afraid of the parts of ourselves that we don't think the world can handle, we get stuck. We create our own hell and prison that keeps us disconnected. Instead, we can allow ourselves to risk being all of who we are, letting the chips fall, and from there, we start to create new evidence. We will still get misunderstood, mis-interpreted, and criticized—all the things. But when we know who we are, confidently embracing that our intentions are good and our best is enough, conflict, old wounds, triggers, and our pain don't get as much power and can eventually stop running our lives. We don't necessarily have to like our pain, but if we're willing to embrace a "bring it on" attitude when it shows up, there's so much power there. There's so much relief, and there's so much life to live the way we've imagined it could be. The only way to get through pain and struggle is to grow through it. We confuse comfort with right for me. Comfort is often unhealthy for us and can reinforce woundedness. Different is difficult and uncomfortable, but that does *not* make different bad.

Have you ever caught a glimpse of the fire in your eyes? I promise it's still there waiting for you to stoke it. The fire in you isn't going to burn anyone. Your soul is meant to be on fire. That light and flame is who you are. You can't put it out. But we try, don't we? We try to simmer ourselves down. We put our souls and dreams on hold. We think the world can't handle our real full-on commitment to being our most fiery selves. Or we think we aren't that fiery or special. Of course, you are. Of course, I am. Of course, we all were born with a flame that's un-extinguishable. We have to be brave enough to pour gas on the fire of our souls. We have to stop being willing to put gas on the fire of our stops and obstacles and fears. You don't get to skip the part where you question and doubt your bigger commitment. Try this on, say out loud, "So what if I don't know how? I'm going for it, all the way. The answers will come. I deserve a life that is well for my soul. I deserve a life that is well for me. The world deserves to meet and experience me healed so I can make my difference."

TAKE THE LEAD

Leadership means going first, leading the way. We seek outside approval and it stops us from leading. We want permission or validation. What's needed is for you to take your life on. Take your life back. Start leading your own life. You wouldn't be here, right now, reading these pages, if you weren't a natural born, inspired leader. Healed leadership is uncomfortable, often, because it demands integrity, but it is oh so very worth it. It takes a commitment to your life and your goals that means that you will pursue them no matter what. This type of leadership is not manipulation or force, it's genuine and doesn't require anyone or anything to be different or to change. We'll discuss this more throughout this book. You learn to focus on what you have control over as a healed leader. Who are you really? Who are you when nobody's watching? Who are you when life is squeezing you? What lights you up? What triggers you? Have you been paying attention? It's in the challenging moments especially, that we have every right to get real, wild, and free, as we step up our healed leadership game. Remember, it's easy to want more when life is easy. If you are not *all in,* allowing your playful and wild side to wake up and start living again beyond the pain, how can you have and create the future you want? Get all in with your pain and you will dance again. Even if it just starts with a head bob, or a shoulder shake, you get to dance.

Music has been one of the most powerful healers in my life. My wish for you is to see your life as a symphony. Listen to the music, and notice your breath. Every note matters. Every emotion matters. Every breath matters. Every instrument matters. The most complex chords, rhythms and tempos are what make life glorious. You hear the music in your soul. See the magic of life, always knowing that there are no wrong notes, no wrong moments, no realities that are less than a perfect symphony. The dance will end, and the music will stop but there will be another song and dance. The music, like life, keeps going. We got disappointed and felt pain so we stopped dancing. The loss of the moment and the gut-wrenching heartbreak became too much to bear. It's so sad. Disappointment and committing to your disappointment and letting your pain win does not have to be the way. When we commit to our suffering that's all that we are left with and breathing in and out, day after day. And that suffering can be so subtle no one would even know, but you do.

Yes, there will be pain as you start to come back to life. It hurts when your foot falls asleep and starts to wake up. The same is true about our lives. When your life has fallen asleep and you begin to wake up to possibility, it can hurt, a lot. I'll be honest, it could be brutally painful at first to face the pain of reality if you've allowed yourself to go on autopilot for years. But just like when your foot comes back to life, it comes back even stronger and the pain is gone, when your life comes fully alive, you can't imagine the bliss waiting for you. Life is meant to be a blast, even when it's not going our way. Some days it's sunny and some days we have natural disasters. It's all just life and emotional weather. You can choose to dance your way through your pain to get to the next song. Don't stop listening to the music in your soul. Sing, even though it hurts. Pain can't last forever. Whatever your dreams are, they are worth living for. Start dreaming again and dream big. The nightmare of your pain can end and another dream will be born if you are willing to risk continuing to live and lead your life beyond the pain, into freedom.

I have a personal rule: I will not go backwards. I fail all the time but I choose to fail *forward*, becoming more of me and experiencing more of life. Let's find out what we are made of and make room for more and more and more. That means allowing failure and risking the bumps and bruises that are a part of growth. Let's trade up in our lives as one chapter ends and another begins. It's my right, and yours, to get the most of your life and that means letting yourself live and run wild while you are here.

FREEDOM AT LAST

If you had no obligations, worries, concerns or "have to's" running you, what would you do with your life? Some of you feel *wild* and free already but do you feel free with your pain? The people in my inner circle now are living wild and free. That wasn't true for most of my life and I don't think it's true for most people. We think it could hurt people, relationships, and our chances if we don't act how we are "supposed" to so that others are comfortable. Here's what I want to tell you, gorgeous one. You are not here in this lifetime to keep other people comfortable or to keep the peace. Your chances can't be ruined. Passion runs through your veins whether you have been paying attention or not. I am not saying that I know what's best for you or how you should live. However, if you want to get the most out of your lifetime, if you believe that life is precious, that life is beautiful, that people are beautiful, if you see the value of getting messy, falling down, getting back up, and digging in so that you can grow and thrive—then *I am talking to you.*

Who do you love that you watched play their life small? Did you see that person and think to yourself, *Good job playing small! Good job being less than who you are!?* Or, did you think, *Come on, be more! Go for it! Shine!?* My guess is that your thoughts leaned toward the latter. So why do we tame ourselves when we want those we love to be the most of who they are? To fit in? To hide? To feed our unworthiness? Or, are you someone who wants those you love to play their lives safe? Do you think those you love need protection from the world? We all in some way, shape or form, try to protect ourselves and each other. But what if we weren't born to be tamed? You were born to be as much of a game changer and difference maker as you can be. What would happen if you gave up playing small? Let yourself grow and live more freely than the ones you saw as stuck but love with all of your heart.

The words "be realistic" make me ill. Now, am I an idealist? Absolutely. Am I a dreamer? Obviously. Am I scared? Daily. Am I wanting to protect my heart? Not anymore. My vision of a life of freedom is clearer than my doubts. What needs to happen for you to get clear, willing, and committed to living wild and free? Once you get that you *are* a wild one, my wish for you is that you'll start to *own it.* Work it.

Love it. No more of your pain running the show called your life. Your pain isn't the main character, you are. What if your free side is your best side? So what if it's not normal and they won't get it? They aren't the ones with your life at stake. I don't mean to shatter your hopes of approval. Never mind, I *do* mean to shatter your hopes of approval. Are you approving of you? Probably not if you are trying to tame your inner wild child. The world can handle it. Be wild. Be you. And you may just lose some emotional pounds and drop your heavy burdens along the way.

GET SUPPORT

In your most inspired reality, who would you have in your corner? A coach, mentor, a solid inner circle and seminars are my personal go-to's in all seasons of my life. Not just in crisis. Crisis is really just waking up, like being born. You may be in a personal crisis right now. Get connected and get support. Lean into your personal hell with support so that you can be reborn and life now can begin. We can get support and start to grow. The next season of your life begins *now*. And then you can catch upsets quicker and quicker before crisis level pain forces your hand.

Imagine a world where you are living free and you are supported by a circle of people who want you to win. What if the problem is not that people are not on board? What if the real issue is that you are not clear about your big wants and that you will do whatever it takes to get them? You have to know what you want first. You have to be able to see it. You have to be able to taste it. You have to want it so much that you will do whatever it takes, as long as it takes, to get it. You have to give up waiting for a guarantee before you go for it, including waiting for the right people to get in your corner. You are in charge;

they'll show up, the most aligned support, to help once you get clear that you are going to do whatever it takes and be who you would have to be to make it happen.

Haters. Judgment. Criticism. Questions. Self-doubt. Wanting to quit and/or wanting to give up. It can all show up as you get more real and in more powerful, healed leadership of your life. I'm not saying that because you deserve it—you don't. I'm saying leaders get put under scrutiny but it can get to a point where you don't take the opinions of the world on as a metric of how well you are doing. Let your ability to check in honestly with yourself about whether or not you have done your best be the metric. The more you see all without thinking it means "I can't," and without fear, the lighter you will be and the faster your goals will come to you—believe it! Your life goals are on their way. Living on autopilot and in fear of the absolutely guaranteed "life requiring more and more commitment from you moments" on the way to your goals, no longer have to stop you, stifle you, and tame you. Get unstoppable. Know that it's normal to have your freak-out moments. It's not that you have the wrong dream or goal when life blindsides you or throws you a curve ball; it's simply that life is testing your commitment to what you said you wanted and who you said you were going to be. Our commitment gets tested. We don't get tested. Obstacles allow us to up our commitment game. They are not a sign to stop. They show us how committed—or not—we are. When you want to quit, tap into your wild side and dance and live louder!

THE CORNFIELD

I run wild in the cornfields starting at about age eight. I sing, dance, and play in these cornfields. The sky's the bluest and brightest when I'm alone with the corn and myself. There are cornfields surrounding the house I'm growing up in. They know my stories and more about my emotions than maybe anyone. Weekend after weekend I find refuge in the cornfields. As I get older, I walk for hours through the fields and along the train tracks (not a good idea). There is a creek behind the tracks and I love it here. The water strokes my hair and my soul. I am safe. I am outside. I am free. In the cornfield is a massive and magnificent tree. In my mind, this tree is stronger than anything else in my life. It withstands all of the storms that happen both inside and outside of my house and the cornfield is home to both of us. When the cornfield holds me there is no fear. I am enough. I can be myself. I let myself run wild and free in these fields. I pretend I am Punkey Brewster, my version of what it means to be carefree and happy. I can be that too under that tree surrounded by cornfields that keep me safe.

It's important to remember that it hasn't always been so painful. There was life before emotional hell and there is life after. I'm going to ask you to be brave right now. I want you to dig deep and imagine a time when it didn't hurt. What is your moment? When was it? Where were you? What did it feel like? Who were you with? What did it smell and taste like? Go there.

Somewhere along the way I let the fear of it hurting so much, hurting too much, and the fear that my emotional pain would never end become paralyzing. But there were moments in the midst of hell where all was truly well. I was safe with me and God in those cornfields. I could go there, sneaking off like a spark coming off of a fire, when I could. We forget to seek refuge in what worked once upon a time. When did you stop knowing how to get back to you as a wild and free soul, the you not consumed by and riddled with emotional pain? We have access to the most vibrant side of ourselves all the time.

For me, I go back in my mind to the cornfields. For so long I thought I could only feel how I wanted to feel and be who I wanted to be alone in the cornfields. I don't know what the moment was when I stopped going there, into the me that I wanted to be, but once I stopped I lost a part of me. But only temporarily. I thought it was those fields that had me running wild. I didn't realize I could live how I was living in those fields all the time. I didn't get, yet, that being the wild and free version of myself could be the rule and not the exception. It was just me in those fields, giving myself permission. To play. To laugh. To sing.

When have you felt the most free? Go back there in your mind. Know that if you could feel free then, you can feel free now. If you've never felt free, or can't remember ever feeling free, what have you imagined and fantasized feeling wild and free would be like? How would it feel? What would you be wearing? What would you be doing? Imagine the sensations. What I know without a doubt, is that your wild side is in you and it's your right to live free. If we have been wild and free before, or even if you can only imagine what feeling wild and free would feel like, you have the power to step into being that version of yourself in the life you have now. If you can't think of anything just find one thing that makes you feel lighter. It could be a favorite flower, your favorite song or painting, just find something that you feel connected to and give yourself permission to feel lighter. We think circumstances need to change for us to get free. It starts with how you are being and who you are being. For example, being rigid (how some people are being) doesn't allow for freedom. Following other people's rules (who some people are being), maybe even your parents rules as an adult can feel limiting and like a trap. Freedom can start now. And yes, your life will change. And yes, it may feel like it's getting worse before it gets better. Some people may go away. But in the meantime, you can choose now to let your hair down.

It wasn't the cornfields at all that had me feeling the way I wanted to feel. Who we are being and how we feel on the inside makes us feel alive, not anything outside of us. On the other side of the pain is freedom and your wild side gets a chance to sing. When we make it the world's job to fulfill us, we lose our way. The world will never, ever be safe enough for you to relax into feeling your way through your pain so you can get to the other side of it. And there *is* another side of it. If you will design your life in a way that is well and healthy for you. And if you will remember what life can feel like when you are no longer willing to let the pain win. You are stronger. You are bigger, more badass, and more equipped than anything that hurt you or is still hurting you. It won't kill you to feel it—it's killing you *not* to. Please, one tear at a time, one glimmer of hope at a time, if that is what it takes, let your life begin to work for you. You deserve to have a great life, a well life, and a free life. You can set up a happy and healthy life for yourself so that you can be of greater service to the world. Why not have what you want?

Journal EXERCISE

- When did you decide it hurt too much to feel?
- What is living in self-protection mode costing you?
- What is the cost of you not healing through your pain?
- What is your creative outlet?
- What is well for you now?
- Who is in your support system?
- What do you know you need to let go of about how you are living now to make room for more?
- What would life be like if you lived as a free bird?
- What is your next vulnerable step?
- What is the next big dream that you are committed to living into and creating for yourself?

Chapter Four

THE HABITS

You don't need help because you aren't helpless.
You need support that believes you can make those
impossible healings and wildest dreams your reality,
and you need new habits.

OLD HABITS DON'T HAVE TO DIE HARD

When I get on my knees and throw up it feels awesome. Like really awesome. It feels awesome because I feel powerful. I want to get my pain out. It also feels like erasing my past. I am carrying so much fear and emotional pain. I try to be sneaky so my little daughter won't know what I'm doing. I live in Las Vegas. It's time to pick my kindergartner up from school. I get in the car, turn on the radio and turn up the volume. Katy Perry's "Firework" is playing and I start singing at the top of my lungs.

Then I cry uncontrollably. I had eaten a cupcake right before I left to pick up my daughter. I'm scared about the calories but really I just want relief. The cupcake didn't make me feel better. I want to feel better but I also don't want to feel. This is the current story of my life. I am singing, thinking about the cupcake, and the tears just fall. I'm terrified that the tears won't stop but I let them come as I drive into a parking lot. Shamefully, I open the car door and, one foot in front of the other, I step into the grossest Vegas gas station there is. Heading into the bathroom I know exactly what my plan is. It's conscious. It's a choice: I'm choosing to throw up before I get my daughter from school and it's time to put my Super Mommy face on. I keep a toothbrush in my purse to use in case of emergencies like this. But the toothbrush isn't working. Nothing comes up, probably because the only thing I had eaten all day was that cupcake.

Next my thoughts tailspin into the narrative that I can't even get my eating disorder right. I'm not a binger. I am starving myself and then I throw up whatever I eat. I'm furious that I can't throw up and feel like both a failure and a crazy person. I am committed to hating myself and hating my life. *Is this rock bottom,* I wonder? The smell of this Las Vegas bathroom. The taste of this old and dirty toothbrush. The walls and floor and this scene is my life. I am like a caged animal. Finally, I throw up the cupcake and it seems all of the possibilities that I really want, and I surrender with abandon into my pain. Temporary solace. Now it's time to dry my tears. I carefully put my toothbrush back in my purse and somehow put one foot in front of the other and get back in my car. Breathing in and breathing out, I drive to pick up my kid and slowly fall back into a fake trance to get through that day.

Avoiding emotional pain, hating myself, and refusing to look in mirrors and at cameras never felt like habits, but they were. I was so good at avoiding myself on a soul level for so long that it became my normal. It never occurred to me that I was defending and committed to my hellish relationship with myself. I never thought that it could be better or transform. It just was what it was. What I know now is that we learn our bad habits, we're aren't born with them. We saw it somewhere from someone who saw them from someone else. This is so important. We watch, listen, learn, and repeat. And then our self-destructive habits are there to protect us. They become a part of us that we are afraid to let go of because we don't know that we can survive without them. Worse, we don't know who we are without them.

But how do we know whether or not a habit is "bad" for us? For starters let's start calling our bad habits old habits because they aren't working anymore. And let's make it simple, again not easy but simple. Here's a hack, if what we think, say, and do is leading us deeper and deeper into self-destruction, then it's just not working. A quick fix is not the same as a cure or real solution. Instant gratification is never going to lead to new long-term healing or healthy results.

One of the worst bad for me habits I've defended and lived on purpose that has kept me insecure, full of fear, and in deep emotional pain has been the way I talk to my body. I was vindictive, for decades. On the street most people saw me and would describe me as loving, kind, and maybe even soft. They didn't hear the voices in my head though: *Rebeccah, look at that gut. Those thighs. How could anyone love you? You're fucking disgusting. It's your fault, body. You are failing me, again.* The conversations pretty much got worse, not better, from there. And my body responded. How does your body respond to how you talk to it? Mine tried to tell me, *Ouch!* But I kept the self-loathing going. My body loved me anyway. My heart continued pumping. My lungs expanded and took in oxygen, all while I was a total asshole to myself. But it was a habit—a lifeline. Habits are what we do on autopilot. We don't think, we just do what we know. We also do what we've seen. We will only create new habits when our habits get more painful than they are useful. Our habits serve us and who we are now in the life we have now. But do we want a new experience as we come back to life? This means adopting *new* habits. Did you get that? Your habits are useful until they aren't anymore. But have faith: you absolutely have what it takes to develop healthier habits that feed the life you want now.

Okay. Before we get too deep into where our old, bad for us habits come from, let's just admit that we all have moments and phases of our lives where what we do isn't helping us get what we want. Wanting it, whatever "it" is, by the way, is never going to be enough for you to actually get what you say you want. And from there we have to start committing to becoming who it takes to be the person who gets the goal and crosses the finish line. If you aren't where you want to be you need new habits and a new commitment, not a new goal. I once had a client ask me if it was OK to just give her goals a plan B. Our goals do not need a plan B. We need new habits and commitments to close the gap between where we are and where we want to be. Plan B on your goals feels like failure and reinforces self-doubt. It's a maybe it will happen, maybe not attitude that keeps you far, far away from where you want to be. If you can see what you want, if you have a dream, or even if you just want more but have no clue what to do next, please know that with the right habits, you can get there if you bet on yourself, burn the option that the dream won't happen, commit to the life you want and refuse to give up. More on this later.

We settle for the "lesser of the losses" because we saw the people who raised us settle as a habit, instead of committing to actually achieving their goals. We allow ourselves to wait because we saw people waiting as a habit, instead of taking a risk and going for it. We surrender to a world of feeling and believing we can't get what we want and then we can't breathe. We put us on hold while we still have life left. Come on! There has got to be a better way. I think that we can literally think that we have no options in the moments that feel impossible. There is not only one world, the one where we manage our way through reliving what we know, saw, learned, and soaked up that exists—talk about brutal—there is a world full of abundance and possibility happening right now and always.

So where do our self-sabotaging and self-sacrificial ways come from? They really are habits but we're not born playing them out. Here's the tea. We saw them. We survived using them. We rely on them. We know they work to help us avoid pain, heartbreak, and failure. The bitch of it is that they also keep us in pain, heartbreak, and experiencing failure because we don't know with certainty that we could survive without them. We don't want to let go of what we know we can survive because we don't trust we will survive beyond the life we know now and grew up living. But how sad to live our childhoods on repeat with different characters in different costumes without blazing the new trail of possibility that we have everything we need to design and engineer.

It's a heavy burden living in a world where we're committed to believing that we are "less than capable." We have our survival habits, and then we play out our childhood pain with innocent bystanders. What I mean by this is we'll say to someone in our life now what we could never say to the people who broke our hearts. We listen for evidence from the people we love to support our bad habits and biggest hurts, fears, and insecurities about ourselves.

Our bad habits are not new, they started young. And because we were kids, we didn't have the language or the voice to be able to say to those caring for us: here is what I need, here is what I want, here is how I am feeling. *We didn't have the ability to check in and check it out when someone said something that hurt, to find out whether or not they meant what we thought we heard.* So we've played out our pain as adults, carrying our habits like a badge of honor, like they are another appendage on our bodies, and we struggle. Then the downward spiral just continues and gets deeper and darker while we feel worse and worse.

What if we created a new habit of taking ownership of our insecurities? For example, I am a lot. The more of me, the better. I have a lot to say. I feel intensely. I love hard. I give my all every day of my life. It's a lot. I'm a lot, and finally, I am proud of all of that. Where we need to be careful is in looking for reasons to shut ourselves down or make ourselves smaller. Wanting more and trying won't lead to change. Defending our obstacles and limitations will only lead to more defeat. Pay more attention to whether or not you are looking for reasons to shut down or reasons to open up, as the best of you and watch miracles start to bloom all around you.

Another idea for a new habit is to use our obstacles as the reason to keep going. Meet yourself. Be the one who can move through the obstacles, because you have what it takes. The habits that keep us from moving through our obstacles have kept us alive and safe so far (or so we think). They have also kept us small. Where are you dimming yourself and dumbing yourself down? We have to identify what isn't working before we can put something new in place. If not now, when? We get into the habit of defending our stuckness and it costs so much. I'm asking you to please start to pay attention to where you do this and how often and in what ways you dim you, the best of you, to defend your pain and survival.

You always have control over paying attention. You won't be perfect, that's fine, that's great, just do your best to be awake, aware, and conscious of the habits that don't serve you anymore who you are being and how you are living. The habits that are working should be kept; the habits that are new may feel scary and uncomfortable, or they can feel liberating. Either way, you come back to life more and more. Every bad habit you think you have has served you in some way and the moment you realize those habits no longer serve, that right there is a miracle.

As an example, here are some of my past bad habits around self-care:

- Avoiding mirrors.
- Restricting food/obsessing about food/guilt and shame around food/crash diets.
- Allowing myself to only get four hours of sleep.
- Avoiding sex or needing sex to gain a sense of control.
- Over-exercising (self-punishment).
- Comparing myself to other women, especially the women in my family.
- Needing approval to feel desirable and "good enough."
- Modeling in front of my daughter stress and disgust about myself.
- Not listening to my intuition and my body's primal signals.
- Negative/toxic self-talk.

Now how could I suggest that these habits have served us and could be helpful? There are several reasons why. First, our habits worked at some point. They definitely work to keep us smaller and comfortable. Our habits also help us see clearly what is *not* going to get us closer to where we want to be. They help us see where we can default to perceived safety and comfort instead of growth and new experiences. They help us to stay connected to or a victim to who we learned it from. Finally, they can help us identify our "go-to strategies" that prevent us from being who we really are.

It takes courage to allow ourselves to want what we don't know really is possible for us. Anything we don't have that we want is because we don't believe we can have it—yet–period. Something is in the way. A big part of what is in the way are our stuck emotions but also our "old" habits. Once we see this, we can correct our course. Disclaimer: once we wake up, we can't go back to sleep, at least not permanently. It hurts to try to go back to life before awareness and before hope of possibility. It hurts to stay stuck in the dark.

Better news: once you can clearly identify your bad habits you can choose to step into an *opposite* commitment. For example, instead of staying committed to my top ten self-care "bad" habits, I have committed to:

- Looking in and facing mirrors.
- Eating well and confidently fueling my body.
- Allowing myself to get eight hours of sleep.
- Leaning into, participating in, initiating, and receiving sex in a way that honors me.
- Exercising because I want to and because it feels good.
- Focusing on personal integrity and whether or not I am coming from a place of fear or possibility.
- Feeling desirable and connected to my sexuality.
- Modeling for my daughter self-love and body compassion.
- Connecting to my body and listening to my intuition.
- Loving and compassionate self-talk.

When you can identify what you don't want and what doesn't work, you discover what would work instead, even if you feel like you don't have the answers, yet. Our old bad habits get us closer to what is needed and necessary for us to be the person it takes to get over, under, and around whatever inevitable obstacles show up. Our habits and underlying safety nets can keep us further away from who we want to be and who we really are if we're not careful. Those old habits at one point in your life were the best you could do, and need to be honored. If we won't honor ourselves at our perceived worst, how can we ever become our best selves and honor how far we've come? All of my years avoiding my gifts and committing to shame give me clarity now around how important it is to honor my life and my capacity for growth and healing.

Once you are awake to these old habits, you get to choose. This is powerful! Once you put it together that you weren't born with a severe distaste for yourself you can change your mind and your habits. See how this works? Warning: if you now know better and continue to do the old habits that you know will keep you suffering, then you are now powerfully choosing and get to keep your pain. This is hard to grasp but if you take on total responsibility for your choices and how they are affecting you every day of your life, you'll get *closer to free.*

Another benefit of our old normal bad habits is we get to see how we play them out to fit in with others. There is nothing more deadly for your soul than selling out to fit in. Fitting in isn't your job. Setting your life up to fit in with you is your job. How will you ever fit in with you if you won't commit to new habits?

The old habits we default to gave us comfort and a way to cope at one time. They may even continue to make you feel safe or bring an illusion of control. The problem is, people set themselves up all the time to sabotage themselves so that they can fail on their own terms. Sabotage yourself all you want, but I'm telling you that there is another way. You gain so much control once you choose to strive to commit to creating a new internal reality for yourself now.

One more consideration that I want to throw at you is that in coming back to life, you get to grow beyond the habits and choices that you grew up with. Just because you may not have seen something done before, like falling madly, crazy, deeply in love with yourself or someone else, or having your own business or that camp on the lake, or your dream of making a difference in the world, doesn't mean that it can't happen for you. We often won't let ourselves grow past what we know based on our family of origin and our inner circles. If you won't grow fully into your life, then you lose. Do I *know* that living fully free, healed and inspired is what should happen for people? No. I am not saying this is the right way that should be imposed on people. I'm just talking to the people reading this at home, or on a plane, or in the bath, who *want to live* beyond their comfortable habits that make them want to stick needles in their eyes. Dramatic much? Yes. That's me. I get dramatic to prove points. I won't apologize for it.

Some of you are reading and thinking, Wow, I can use what I have done that hasn't worked to move forward now? Some of you are seeing that you can go beyond what you've known as normal, or just the way things are. You can grow beyond your day to day and the day to day of those you love. It doesn't mean that the day-to-day peeps are bad or wrong. They are beautiful too. It just means choosing for yourself how you want to live. Notice what has and has not worked. Notice who you are showing up as in comparison to how you want to show up and who you want to be. Practice stepping into how you want to live, especially in the moments where it feels like all is lost and there just isn't another way. You are the way. The flow is coming. You've just got to get your pain out of the way. Show up and lead. Show up and live. Now that we have seen this and know the collateral damage attached with our bad habits, we can stand for talking straight with ourselves, with a new commitment to life.

Commitment and compassion can become your new normal. It's more and more becoming mine. You know the cost of being asleep at the wheel of your own life. Now we can all knock it off and love ourselves and each other more. You can create new habits, using what you've learned about what takes you in the opposite direction of where you want to go, as the path to get there.

We have so many habits that keep us safe, small, and hurting. Which are yours? Here are some more examples to get you thinking. The list goes on and on. Hint: your personal bad habits are any way that you are trying not to feel those emotions.

- Being unclear about what takes care of you
- Disconnection from our bodies, our emotions, ourselves, and other people
- Internalizing fear
- Punishing ourselves and others
- Codependent behavior
- Reacting instead of leading
- Wanting to be wanted so bad that we fake who we are
- Self-sacrifice to get love
- Being a workaholic
- Affairs
- Addictions
- Substance abuse
- Alcohol abuse

- Violence, verbal or physical (experiencing or doing it)
- Spending too much
- Escaping and numbing out
- Smoking cigarettes
- Too much TV
- Cheating yourself or others in any way
- Overeating
- Restricting food
- Over-exercising

It's time to start letting go of your self-inflicted protective layers that hold your soul hostage. When you let go and it starts to feel like the bottom is falling out, that's because it is. Let it happen. I know it's scary but when we hold on to what makes us feel safe, we trap ourselves. Do you want to live trapped in your own life? If you do feel trapped, it's time to let you out. Let the chips fall. You can survive the fallout of you showing up to your own life, meaning whatever falls away needed to. Can you survive the prison sentence of keeping yourself trapped in a life you hate, all covered up? The answer is yes, but I don't think that's living.

When you let yourself "out" and take the covers off, one layer at a time, you'll start to breathe again. No matter what our life looks like now, we will experience loss and heartbreak. That's life. Life also offers us wins, big wins, and big, open-hearted miracles and memories. Before now we wouldn't give up our old bad habits because we might lose. The only thing we actually lose is anything that's no longer in alignment with who we are now and the life we want now. Guess what, we're losing anyway when we hold on so tight. Go ahead and grieve, let go, that's living. Life changes when we go for it. Change means more is coming, it's on its way to you right now. Risk heartbreak. The heartbreaks are just you healing, getting more real, and getting more free.

EXPOSED

How crazy is it that because our hearts got broken early, we don't want to experience that again? Another habit we can choose to let go of—I got hurt, so now I protect and shut down my heart. Come on. Come back into you because you deserve to belong to yourself in this lifetime. We are taught to associate love and being ourselves with heartbreak and a belief that it's going to hurt too much to expose who we are to the world and those we love. What if instead we understand that what hurts the most is withholding who we could be and that there's never a good reason to let that happen. And know you will keep evolving. The world doesn't know about you yet and there are so many more versions of you to come that the world and life can't wait to embrace.

You are not crazy. You are not broken. Your heart has been broken. You have been in a mess. You are not a mess. The getting messy part of healing is the "magic" it takes to come alive! We want the pain to melt away like magic. It's going to melt off, one tear at a time. One smile at a time. One laugh at a time. One workout at a time. One breath at a time. One good night's sleep at a time. One day of you taking the covers off of you at a time.

HYSTERICS WEREN'T WORKING

Crying isn't my favorite thing to do, but when I feel threatened it's natural to fall into hysterical tears. I've been doing personal growth for years and I think I'm growing. I don't ever want to be angry so I prefer crying. I'm in coaching certification training and I'm having a moment where I am

confronting an assault that happened in my mind and I become hysterical.
That's the work, right? I'm used to this. It's not that bad. I will feel to heal
and it will all be okay soon. Except, the trainer stops what she is doing looks
me in my eyes and says, in front of the entire group, "I don't believe you."
I'm shocked. Aren't I supposed to cry? And then I'm even more shocked
because I've stopped crying. Now we are just looking at each other, a
standoff. My tears were a habit. These were victim tears—not healing tears.
Who knew that there was a difference? This is the moment that I see that
there is a whole next level of emotional healing. Going through the motions
crying anytime I was upset was a habit that didn't serve me anymore. It
was time to take it deeper, and I was grateful that I was about to learn how.
Being hysterical was not how I wanted to get attention anymore. Getting
real was what I wanted and this was real. I could handle real. A new habit
of committing to "getting real" was born.

SIT WITH "IT"

Have you ever had a moment where you didn't recognize yourself
in the best way? Where you broke through and met a next-level you?
Those moments get to be more and more your reality—if you want
that. In those moments, discover what you tried that had worked and
create some new routines and habits. And then you will sit with and
get closer to the old bad habits so you can replace them with something new. Then take all the new that's working and make it your life.

The moment we decide to move forward with a goal in life it starts
to happen. The moment we decide to lean in to what isn't working so
that we can create and explore what could and would work instead,
we get more powerful. We must stop covering up our stuck fear. Fear
can be tricky because it doesn't always look like you or someone else

shaking in their boots. Fear is an energy. Fear can be as subtle as a snake in the grass that you didn't see coming. You can know stuck fear is haunting you if you aren't happy or blissful or peaceful. This life, for me, is about getting happy, blissful, peaceful, joyful, and most of all free, even in the darkest and dustiest corners of my memories. Let's start a movement together. A movement of living free and inspired even with our pain, even with our pasts, even with the odds stacked heavily against us. Let's start a new habit. Why? Because we can.

What I've learned is that my best is enough. And just keep going. There's nothing to be so ashamed about, or embarrassed by, or convinced that you can't get beyond. It's all healable and your best is enough. Just stay in the game called your life. When you are brave enough to face, move through, and conquer the habits that no longer serve you, another level of life awaits and rewards you, every time. At least that has been my experience.

Journal EXERCISE

- How do you numb out?

- What are you afraid would happen if you began to take off the covers and let the world see you?

- If you took off the covers what would you be leaving behind?

- What does being free mean to you?

- If you took off the covers what would you show to the world?

- Make a list of your top ten bad habits that keep you in survival mode now.

- Make another list of new habits that are the opposite of what you have been doing that will bring you more life.

Chapter Five

THE BODY

Our body is what carries all of our frustration and despair resulting from putting our lives, our love, our joy, and our inspiration on hold.

When I get married the first time, I am six months pregnant and terrified. I am so excited about the baby but it honestly feels like I'm playing house, with no earthly idea of what I am doing. I am twenty-three. My mother gives me a wedding gift. It is the most gorgeous lingerie I have ever seen. Gorgeous white lace with flowers and a corset. It is beautiful. There is, however, one gigantic problem: it is a size 2. I am six months pregnant. My cute body at that time pre-pregnancy, had never been smaller than a size 6 and I am pregnant and already feeling like my body isn't mine. The fear of the baby weight and a new marriage and the pregnancy has induced acne all over my body and I feel like the walls are closing in on me every day. The lingerie feels like a gut punch followed by three left hooks to my jaw. My body has never been the right size in my mind. I wish I could send my body back and get a new one. This is so confusing for me. I'm determined to get to a size 2. That must be the magic size.

After my first daughter is born I somehow seemingly easily and successfully lose the baby weight and get down to 25 pounds less than I was before I got pregnant. I achieve the ultimate goal of a size 2 (and actually maintain it for four or five years pretty easily). It felt like my body was finally "right." A miracle, and yet, I'm devastated to find that I still feel fat, and every day I am afraid of gaining the weight back. I was running like a maniac and counting Weight Watchers points like someone whose life depended on staying a size 2. I think I actually believed that my life did depend on staying a size 2. But everything fell apart anyway. I got cheated on in my marriage. I got hit. I left with a two-year-old who was about to turn three with her whole life ahead of her. But my life felt like it had ended along with the marriage. I had stayed thin. Wasn't that enough? My body had failed me again.

The tears would not stop. I couldn't breathe. My two-year-old was sleeping in her room and I didn't know how I would provide for her, care for her, or keep going. I wasn't sure how the hell I would get off the floor. I wasn't sure how I was going to make it through the night. But the voices in my head were mostly screaming at me, *If you weren't so fat this wouldn't have happened to you. Your husband wouldn't have cheated if you weren't so fat. Your husband wouldn't be calling you names or violent if you weren't so fat. Your husband would have been good to you if you weren't so fat.* I was about 110 to 115 pounds at the time. I felt as hard and frozen as the floor that I was a puddle on. It was my body's fault, right? Less food. Back to purging. More trying to succeed in spite of my body followed.

We think we need more things, better clothes or a new job, a new marriage, a new city, new friends, or a new body, and then life will work. Or maybe that was just me. I've tried them all. New states, new careers, new cars, new diets, new hair, more makeup, less makeup, new men, new clothes. None of it healed the heartbreak or the fear my body held on tight to. We can't hide our pain, especially not from our body; it knows too much. When we try to hide it spreads like the plague to all of our cells and gets louder.

I've never admitted this but I think after my divorce I decided that maybe there was no point to being thin. Being fat was what had been wrong with me my entire life and getting thin only—to my great shock—felt like life was worse, not better. This was one of the biggest blows to my soul that I'd ever had to face up to at that point. Thin was supposed to solve it all. But the beauty of the shock and horror upon realizing that being thin was never the problem or the solution allowed me to commit more than I ever had before to taking my life back.

We have in fact survived what hurt us when we were young. I understand that you may be hurting now. But have you considered that you may have so many layers of survival covering you up and you may have been so used to neglecting your body and your emotions that you can't see you are just taking it? Taking it meaning what's not good enough and not good for you. STOP. JUST. TAKING. IT. Taking life the way it's been can end, today. Right now.

We live our lives. We get our lives. We can love ourselves and our lives. Some may call you selfish but selfish in the name of getting the most out of your life so that you can be your best for others is a selfish I recommend. We get a very finite amount of time to live and what we live in throughout all of this life is our one body. It's the one thing you've got for life. People spend millions, even billions worldwide to correct physically perceived flaws that are already strictly perfection. It's crazy. Why do we hate our bodies so much? My theory is that it's because our bodies can't deny our emotional experience. Our emotions need to be felt through. Instead, we focus on how we are feeling about our circumstances instead of on how we're truly feeling emotionally and then doing the work to fully feel and experience our emotions. People notice our self-loathing. Our kids, especially, notice. You giving the mirror the death stare does not get past your babies. You standing in the closet crying creates an energetic ripple throughout your home that hits everyone in your home, like lightning.

We aren't happy because we are disconnected from our bodies and when we are disconnected from our bodies we disconnect from our emotions automatically. If you would be willing to admit the truth and embrace that you have never been one pound too much of who you are, both literally and metaphorically, you'd feel lighter, I promise. Over the years my body has changed sizes and its shape more times than I can count. I have also gained and lost more pounds than I can count. For decades I thought my body was separate from myself. I tried to dress it up and get the outfits right so no one would notice my insecurities or the mess that was my life.

Your body *is* you. There is not you and then your body as two separate things. You are one. Your body has been there. It's taken all of you in, all of your choices in, all of your circumstances in, all of your dreams, and all of your emotions in. Your body is the only thing that is yours that no one can take away from you as long as you live. You and that body have got to and can become a team. You and that body have got to end the cold war. You and that body deserve to start partnering your way through life, together, in the way that only you two can pair up.

No more avoiding mirrors and cameras. I know it hurts. I know it hasn't always been easy or fun to live in your skin. But that's just because your emotions have felt too big and too painful, but they aren't. You made it. You are still here. We survive in our bodies and in our lives and forget to live. We suffocate our true essence and try to bury our stories, our pain, our pasts, and our most inspired and healed future gets covered up too. We listen to the bullshit, our own, and others' hateful and fear-based venom. Why? Enough is enough. Stop the madness. It's time to settle into your skin. If you won't settle into your skin, then how will you ever settle into your life?

SELF-SACRIFICE? NOT YOUR FRIEND

Your body knows your whole story. Your body is your representative. Your body is your greatest tool and teacher. *Your body knows.* Your body talks. Your body is your strongest ally and advocate, and it has every answer to every question you've ever had, so please start listening to it. Your body knows what isn't working for you and what is working for you. Stop trying to fit into who you think you have to be. That's the wrong direction. That's a shitty way to live. *Every time we give ourselves up to try and keep what we think we should have or be or do, we allow another piece of possibility for our future to fade away.* Have you ever loved someone so much that you were willing to lose you to try and keep them? Have you ever given up a part of you, your truth, your self-care, your dignity, and sold out for another? If you are sitting at home saying, *No way, not me,* look again. We've *all* been there. Let's talk straight now about self-sacrifice. Why is it called self-sacrifice? Because when you make yourself a sacrificial lamb you give up YOU as you make someone else a priority. The result is you undermining yourself, and training other people that you think you are a piece of shit. Self-sacrifice is not your friend and your body knows, even if you are in denial, and it will rebel.

We do what is most beneficial in every moment. Before you try to tell me that there is no benefit to self-sacrifice and you have no idea why you do it, let's get some perspective. Who have you seen modeling sacrificing themselves for another? So let's talk about self-sacrifice, get real and give it up, please. We learn it. We see it. We think it's love. We think it's protection. We think it's going to keep our relationships intact if we try to fit in with the other person, or the job, or the community, or the friend group. *Wrong!* What happens when we self-sacrifice is we lose the essence of who we are. This means whoever the hell we are trying to relate to is now talking to a robot. No one is home when we give ourselves up. We become fake, going through the motions, alien to ourselves which means no one can really feel, "get," or understand us now. Do you see the collateral damage of refusing to be brave enough to stand in your power? If they can't or won't love you standing in your truth then politely ask them to get out of your way. The lack of love from them isn't a worthiness issue on your part, it's an alignment issue. Again, what's not aligned needs to fall away. Don't sell out to try and keep it. Please don't sell out. Again, your kids are watching. Are you someone who learned that you had to try and fit in, or to be who you are supposed to be? Were you taught to toe the line, or else? These are miserable ways to live. I am boiling down for you exactly why we are so good at suffering. We won't be ourselves; the versions of ourselves that we want to be now and it pisses our bodies off and then our body lets us know. It's real that you might lose people when you get really real. Do it anyway. Your body will thank you and will be healthier for it. Attract your people, places, and things. We don't need people in our lives that dumb themselves down and want us dumbing ourselves down. Love them and know that it's totally okay to let them go.

What if you being alone with you is the best company there is? Full disclosure: peeling the layers of fake you off one at a time isn't exactly pleasurable in moments, but do it anyway and you will eventually get to experience unmatched pleasure because there's nothing about how you are living anymore that isn't good for you. You can get to a place where you only expect and allow what's good for you and true for you to be a part of your experience of life. It won't kill you to get back to your truth even if it feels like you might die if you get that honest and real. No one is going to die. The way you were living that wasn't what you really wanted will die and you will be reborn. It's your right to live in your one life as who you are, the way you want to live, in the body you have now, the way it is now.

You're going to have to work for it, life the way you want it, and your body will help you get there faster because it holds every truth you will ever have. You're going to have to want freedom in your body and in your life more than your pain. Suffering and you need to break up. As you break up, the fear, the anger, the grief, the unknown and the foreign waters will inevitably challenge your sweet, just-the-right-sized ass making room for the joy and excitement that long to be expressed through you. This is all part of the unraveling of who you are *not*, so that who you are can begin to shine through. Allow the unraveling. What you will find on the other side is you.

GOD GAVE YOU A LIFE PURPOSE

Have you ever been caught in a riptide?

The silky smooth kiss of the water softens my fear and makes swimming even in a strong current more doable. I can float. I can breathe. My muscles work. My body is strong. I can hide my pain and the water will hold me and love me. Thank God. I'm fourteen and today I am crossing Lake Ontario with my dad. It might as well be the ocean, especially with the wind today. We are moving our boat to a new marina and it's an all-day trek. It starts out fun and fabulous with me on the bow of the boat listening to my Discman and singing at the top of my lungs. I sing out strength and hope and let the wind brush back my hair and let me be me. I don't know when the storm starts. I don't know how it got so bad so fast. The boat's navigation stops working and I watch my father put on a life jacket. I have never seen him wear a life jacket. That's when I know something terrible is happening. I come in off the bow just in time, carefully, one foot in front of the other. The boat is flooded with water. Each wave pushes and pulls and water comes in from all sides. I suddenly realize that I want to live. *Will we be lost at sea? Am I going to die on a boat with my father?* Hours go by. I am strong and poised and so is he. We don't talk. We hold steady as the boat rocks and the water pounds. Eventually the Coast Guard finds us and guides us to shore. We end up hours from where we intended to dock. In my body I am unsure and unsteady, not knowing whether or not my body will support me as it shakes like a maraca. When the Coast Guard finally guides us close to the dock, my father asks me to crawl onto the bow of the boat, grab a line, jump off and tie us up. I am frozen for a few moments. Then I hear him saying, "It's okay if you're scared. You don't have to do this." But I want to. I want to help get us safely to shore. But I don't know if I can make the jump. I could slip. The storm is strong and the rain is fiercely pouring down like an incessant hammer. The water is so rough. What if I fall in the water and get trapped under the dock, or the boat, or get eaten by the two props spinning around and around, like the fear in my head, with no plan of slowing down or stopping? I take the leap and tell myself that I am strong and I am agile. Somehow, my feet move. I hold steady. The line ends up in my hands and I crawl over the safety bar with almost no room to stand on. I jump from the boat to the dock. It's a big, big jump. I make it! I go into beast mode, tie up the rope like a pro, pull the boat in, then hit the dock on my knees and cry, hard, gasping for oxygen as I slowly come back into my body. I made it. We made it. The boat is okay and we are okay. It doesn't matter how far off course we are; we have what we need to keep going. *We're on life's timetable, not ours,* fourteen-year-old me thinks. Right?

⚮

My body held me that day. My body did what I needed it to do. Think about this—what if our bodies have always been doing what we needed and are capable of following through on the actions that are needed? What if the body knows better how we feel, what we want and what we need more than anything else? Your body is miraculous and unwavering in its ability to keep functioning, thriving, and working hard to heal and get back to homeostasis 24/7. Do you honor that? Do you thank your body? It doesn't give up. It doesn't conditionally love you. It's constantly communicating and listening. The body is in it for the marathon, not the sprint. It's your vehicle to get through your days, weeks, months, years, and decades. It will never try to divorce or leave you, no matter how cruel you are. Our bodies never leave us, until we die. Of course, the hard truth is that the body will eventually give out, but as far as I know, that's not happening in this moment, even if it seems like it's hanging on by the thinnest thread. Your body will carry you. Your body will love and honor you, listening to your every primal need as well as to every word of your self-talk. It holds every memory in every cell and gives you chance after chance to show up for your life at your best every single day your eyes pop open, showing you new opportunity and possibility.

We can't fulfill our life purpose of fully living as and at our best if we're unhappy, feeling fat, depressed, anxious, or waiting to live in any capacity. So many lives end abruptly and young. There are millions who want babies that can't get pregnant. There are terminal illnesses that take people out with no notice or warning. But you are here. You are here in your body and you were born with a purpose. Your body is the vehicle that takes you through life; it's also the vehicle to your life purpose. You were born with a purpose. You were born with a dream and a mission and the ability to leave your unique thumbprint on the world. No one is here on this Earth alive and kicking so that they can be miserable and wish the days away. We get by and we are much too good at it. We try to distract ourselves from going after what we really want and what we know we are meant to do. But no longer: it's time to *live.*

There is a light in you. There is a purpose for your life. The kicker is, you have not peaked yet. The best of your life is not behind you. How do I know that? I choose to believe it. Please know that you could choose to level your life up going into this next season of your life. We can put new gas, more gas, in our inspired aliveness life tanks and use what has and has not worked so far to create the next dream we've got. Creating our dreams is something we get to do since we have been given the gift of life. Your goals and dreams and life purpose won't necessarily make you happy or be the magic answer to all of your problems, *you just get to live your life your way.* Why not make the choice to live your way instead of waiting for a life-changing crisis to give you a reality check?

LET'S TALK LIFE PURPOSE

My strong belief and personal and professional experience have shown me that it's much easier to get real and let our bodies and souls be seen if we have something to look forward to. How many years has it been since you have known why you should get out of bed in the morning? Life purpose doesn't mean that you have to do some "big thing" with your life and it means something different to everyone. There are no rules here. You just get to do with your life what brings you freedom and fun. People ask me why I spend literally every day working on myself. My answer is because I have a blast ironing out the wrinkles of my soul and peeling back the layers of self-protection and fear that have kept me from fully living my life. Why do I want to talk to you, write this book, and speak to as many people as I can about *Coming Back to Life* in the body I have now? Because for me it's a blast! I've spent decades in hell. I don't want to continue living that way. I play a game with myself where with each breath I strive to beat a personal record for more and more freedom, like my life depends on my next best score because the quality of life that I have does. What would be a blast for you? If you had your very own personal genie, how would you want to live? What would you ask for? You need your body to live your life's work. And I believe that we all have our own life's work to do while we're here. We have a body and a life. Now, what will you do with those sacred and precious gifts that are permanently in your possession even when life changes?

I'm looking out my window at the mountains as I write. For most of my life I thought I was supposed to conquer those mountains. But I'm learning that I get to see myself at the top of whatever mountain I face, before I know how on earth I will get up that mountain. I am growing, you're growing too. It can be daunting to think about living and growing in a way where you are living standing at the bottom of the mountain trying like hell to figure out how you're going to get all the way to the top. Back that ass up for a second and consider that you can try the opposite approach. Yes, our goals, especially for many of us our life-purpose work, can be daunting and feel like a big ol' insurmountable mountain. My suggestion is to take the aerial view approach. Don't worry so much yet about how you are going to get there. So many of us won't commit or go for it until we know how it's going to work. We wait until it feels like we've got a slam dunk or have some sort of guarantee, but it's never enough because there are no guarantees. There is just your very real soul, and your very real body, and your very real purpose that all desperately want to be born into your life, authentically. Commit first without having even an inkling of how you are going to arrive at your goal, and baby, you are on your way.

It will look like trial and error. There will be failures but you can still get your groove on and feel and know that your mojo and momentum are in full swing even amidst setbacks. You'll get in full swing, if you are committed. Commitment means doing whatever it takes as long as it takes. Once committed, life *will* be life in all of its seasons, weather, and flavors. Keep going, meeting yourself on a soul level, while you honor your body, committed to purpose and freedom and you will start to feel lighter because you will feel freer even if circumstances haven't shifted or changed, yet.

For many years I wouldn't dream. My focus was survival. I identified with survival mode. I was protecting myself by giving up my right to magical thinking like a child does. My identity protected me, but life really hurt without dreams or purpose. What was needed for me to stay in magical thinking? It was about giving myself permission to allow my identity to be a new one that I chose. I realized I was never going to find myself and that it was time to awaken to what I needed and wanted, creating a new identity that served the life I wanted now.

Until you become BFFs with that body of yours, your life will be in a constant state of war. You won't win that war either. Neither will your body. You may win some battles through distracting yourself through instant gratification or drunken stupors or great sex. Do you want moments or do you want your life? What do you want to do in this lifetime? When you look at the moon, the stars, the ocean, the mountains, the flowers, and the trees, what do you fantasize about? Without your precious, unique body, how can you make any fantasy reality?

Notice your breath and how it fights and works so hard for you. Notice your ability to see or imagine colors, vibrancy, and the beautiful mess of what is in front of you. Listen. No, really listen. We listen to the voices in our heads instead of our bodies. Your body hears everything. Your miraculous body never stops absorbing your environment. We'll trust anything but our body but it's only the body that knows. Let's choose an identity that believes in caring about our bodies.

My coach once said to me that my body was my greatest tool as a coach. I did not believe her and I wouldn't listen at first. Turns out that she was absolutely right. This body has given all to me and to anyone in front of me. For this body I created Rebeccah's support system. I am a cancer survivor. Cancer had me begin a love affair with my body that may be the greatest love story I will have in this lifetime. While I committed to healing cancer, I hired a private yoga therapist, massage therapist, acupuncturist, Reiki master, chiropractor, physical therapist, cranial sacral therapist, personal trainer, naturalist oncologist, and a chef. The massage therapist told me one day that the parts of my body that hurt the most were fighting the hardest for me.

I have work to do in this lifetime. You have work to do in this lifetime. That work doesn't have to be hard. Life doesn't have to be hard. Instead, it can look and feel like ease and flow. We all have a life and we can drive it effortlessly instead of being at the mercy of what life throws our way. We can get as clear as possible, as healthy as possible, and maintain a focus on what it is that we want our lives to be and feel like. We get to live how we want to with purpose that we choose. The most depressed people that I have ever worked with had no purpose and didn't think that they had any talent to offer. The work I want to do is to have a blast with people and heal as much as I can while I'm in this body. Those who want to join me in healing while having fun and feeling free, regardless of circumstance have an open invitation. But the deal is, we can't do any of it without our bodies.

Your body is truly everything. It asks for the bare minimum from you and keeps going. We really test our bodies, don't we? We ignore, reject, belittle, and get so mean to our bodies. I am not the first to say this but I will say it anyway:

When you are tired, sleep.

When you are thirsty, drink.

When you are hungry, eat.

When you are feeling sexual, have great sex.

When your body wants to move, exercise.

And dance. Always dance.

Listen to your body. Listening isn't thinking. Listening isn't anticipating what you need, guessing at what you need, or trying to figure out what you should do next. Listening is getting still and being with you. I do yoga and move almost every day and when it's time to sit in a pose, I can get squirmy. In those moments, I lean in more until I am still enough to listen. We get squirmy in life instead of sitting still and listening. Listen. Let your soul talk through your body. Your soul can't sing if you haven't even let it whisper let alone talk. Your body holds your soul. Your soul holds your secret truths. Your body and soul are one. It knows. It's genius. It's perfect.

One of the strangest realizations that I had after cancer, more about that soon, was that I still wouldn't want a different body. I genuinely wouldn't trade. No way. This is the body that knows me. This body has been with me, fighting for me, letting me hate it and love it, and it's never stopped loving me. I mean it that I wouldn't want another body, even doctors have told me me that cancer could come back at stage 4. Cancer could come back. The benign tumor in my brain could grow. The benign tumors in my liver could grow. I have all kinds of reasons to hate, dismiss, or try to disown my body. But I have chosen, now that I'm in my forties, to honor and love it up. I admit that all of these realizations and this new way of living *through,* instead of *in spite of,* my body are recent. I can tell you, however, that I'm not going back. I choose my phenomenal body.

Your life purpose may seem out of reach. Commit to who and what you will have to become to get all the way there. Commit to creating the identity that will take you there. I promise that you have all the answers that you'll ever need in your amazing body. *That* body. It will tell you everything you've ever wanted to know if you will connect to, love, and honor it. From there you've got to listen, find your truth, live your truth and then you are free.

Think about every accomplishment you have ever had. Your body helped you get there. You didn't get there in spite of your body. You got through every obstacle and came out the other side because of your body and it's unwaveringly loving and consistent support. I know you have a vision and a dream for your life, even if you have buried it deep along with your ability to connect to and listen to your body. Your body IS what will allow you to make it from where you are now to where you want to be. Please start listening. Please start thanking your body. Please stop misusing your body and checking out of your body.

In the moments where we check out I think it's because we think we'll die if we don't. I am fairly certain that when and if we are checking out of our bodies there is a real reason why. What I mean is, past pain or fear is being reactivated. This why, however, is irrelevant and does not need to be defended. We are bigger and bolder than that pain or that real fear. Remember, the more we identify with and defend our habits and survival strategies that keep us where we are instead of moving toward being fully alive, the more we repeat history day after day and wait for and miss our lives. You won't die if you go for it, and when you die I hope you will die knowing you went for it. I know this may sound harsh or drastic but come on, this is the only life you've got now. It may be the only life you get. Your body has and holds *all* of your truth, prayers and every answer to all of your questions. Your body also has the most incredible capacity to forgive, love, and heal. I believe that our bodies want us free and flying as high as we can to the top of our lives. We don't have control about how much time we have in our bodies, but we do have control over how we treat our bodies in the time we are given. We all have what it takes to summit each and every mountain but if we don't believe that first we won't be able to experience the views.

I will never forget the feeling of my feet landing on the dock that stormy day and my hands knowing the way. Once you begin to see your body as a miracle that only honors you no matter how you show up, instead of as the enemy, your body brings you closer to being free every moment of your life.

So this all sounds good in theory, right? End the war with the body. Of course. Stop neglecting your body. Well, duh. Self-inflicted cruelty and abuse to the body will only hurt you and keep you in struggle. No kidding. Eat, sleep, drink water, have sex, exercise, meditate, dream, all super great and essential ingredients to living our best life and . . . we won't, or we haven't, but we can start. My suspicion is that at least one of these things you won't do, yet. Which one is your Achilles' heel? Why you "won't" doesn't matter. Will you be the person who chooses to really live from now on? That's the question.

For me, this looks like my life purpose. Taking on life and every drop of current kryptonite as I notice it. Life-purpose work which can seem like an insurmountable mountain, even more so than taking on bodywork and self-care. Baby steps. Start with connecting to your body and from there, in due course you'll get access to your life purpose, whatever that truth is in the moment that you're finding yourself in. It will evolve and transform, let it. Just keep finding and living into what's important now. Keep it simple.

THE RAPE

I was having nightmares. At night, anxiety and depression took over. The sweat I would wake up drenched in was freezing. I had four roommates, but I was so alone. It was scary to fall asleep and I was afraid to wake up. I was severely depressed. Clinically depressed to the point where the therapy team I was working with suggested hospitalization and medication. What was wrong with me? I would start crying and like clockwork the tears would last five hours every time. Literally five straight hours of bawling my eyes out in a sitting. I took the medication but refused to go to the hospital. Instead I went to therapy three days a week and read the book, *The Courage to Heal,* by Ellen Bass.

A friend in college had been raped. As we got closer and I heard more about her story I realized that I had also been raped in high school and at night I was having flashbacks. I didn't even know what a flashback was before this. The confusion was real because it didn't "feel" like rape. I knew him. We were together. I trusted him. But one day, in his house, where I had been so many times before, he was more aggressive. I said no in the living room. He responded by throwing me over his shoulder and throwing me down on his bed where I had also been so many times before. The word no escaped my lips over and over but he wouldn't stop. I didn't understand what was happening. *Was this really happening?* It hurt. I was furious but my rage came out as helpless tears. Eventually I kicked him off of me and ran out of the house. I left my shoes there, running barefoot a mile down the road to another friend's house.

My bare feet felt the pavement but I was out of my body and couldn't feel a thing. It was just a few minutes but I didn't realize the impact until much later. I ended the relationship after that but for four years it never occurred to me that I had been raped. It only occurred to me that that was not the person I wanted to be with. My body was used to taking it. I was used to blaming myself. I didn't see it. The pain was too much. I didn't want to feel the heartbreak or my anger. My body wouldn't let me forget until I healed and addressed what I had buried. I didn't understand at the time that's how it works.

Realizing that I had been raped had me suicidal. So much came up from even earlier years in my life and I just wanted the pain to stop. I couldn't stop crying. My body was talking but I still wouldn't listen. It took me almost taking my life before I would listen.

YOUR BODY IS YOUR GREATEST ALLY

Your body is what carries all of the frustration and despair that results from putting our lives, our love, and our joy and inspiration on hold.

Your body *knows* all of you. Your body *is holding* all of you. I have spent most of my lifetime at war and absolutely hating myself, and I took it out on my body. My body took the fall only every single time my heart broke or I had a meltdown or things didn't go my way, until cancer. It took cancer as a wakeup call to force my hand to end the war and to begin to see, love, and honor my body for the first time. Cancer came and I knew if I kept hating my body I might as well sign my own death certificate. Were there moments where I blamed my body after getting diagnosed? Yes. Was I furious with my body for not being strong enough to not have cancer? Yes. Talk about emotional cancer that was toxic. I couldn't love my life and get through cancer hating my body. I believe ending the war with my body helped save my life. I made the powerful choice to see my body as innocent and so strong that it could beat cancer. And it did.

Our bodies absorb our shock, heartbreak, disappointment, shame, guilt, fear, anger, terror, all of it. What would life be like if we allowed our bodies to soak up more laughter, freedom, joy, love, hope, gratitude, and forgiveness? Once you win your war with your body you get to have your life. You just have to decide it's worth being wrong about what you fought so hard for so long with your body about. Do you want to be *right* or *free*? It's okay to move on in peace and harmony. Allow your body and your soul to merge and become one. *They already are.*

Your life is waiting. Your calling and purpose is getting closer and it's getting louder. My mission right now is to live inspired, emotionally healed and fully expressed, regardless of circumstances, and to be the megaphone for every person that wants this too. What's yours?

Can you feel it getting closer yet? Your life? Your voice? Your body relaxing into a softness and truth that is and has always been you? Your life purpose is calling and you'll need your perfect body to fulfill it. It's not too late and you are not so flawed that your life shouldn't come full circle and arrive into the free-flowing dance of your life purpose.

Your body will take you there, into your comeback story, and wherever you want to go, today, tomorrow, or even ten years from now, so why wait? If you don't know your "why" yet, don't fret. It will come. Instead of being in the downward spiral conversation about why has life happened the way it has, start with a commitment to getting to the place where you do know "why" you want to get out of bed in the mornings and follow that narrative. What is it that you are living for that's bigger than you, the past and your pain? When we don't have a purpose in life, life becomes monotonous and hard. It's hard enough to face the storms and curveballs and unexpected fall-outs of life that have nothing to do with us. Having a purpose keeps us going, in joy. What other way is there to live that you would choose? Take care of that body and it's all yours for the taking.

Journal EXERCISE

- What do you want to change about your body and your life, and why?

- Where do you sell out and what is the cost?

- What are you asking of your body and are you giving it what it needs to thrive?

- If you had your very own personal genie, how would you want to live? What would you ask for?

- What do you fantasize about? What would be a blast for you?

- What are you living for?

- What is your new promise to your body?

- Who are you going to be and what are you going to do for your body now?

- Write your body a love letter thanking it for its service.

Chapter Six

THE POWER

See beyond what you think will heal the pain. Be willing to grow into your greatness.

I got leveled with a cancer diagnosis when I was thirty-four and seven months pregnant. In my coaching office I am rarely blindsided. It's not that I am always aware enough to see what's coming, but it almost always, at the very least, makes sense to me: people's behavior, where it comes from, what's possible no matter how they feel or how they behave. The cancer diagnosis, however, leveled me. On a Monday. Right before my birthday. Right before I was about to have a baby. I could literally not breathe and could not believe it. But then they told me that I was probably fine, there was a 95 percent chance that the cancer was stage 1. They would just need to mutilate my left arm, where the tumor was, but then I "should" be okay. A tumor? I had a mole. It was a mole. No, it was a tumor. It was malignant melanoma. Knock me over with a feather.

I'm told I'm probably okay. *Probable* is such an interesting word. It's never probable that a disaster is going to happen but they show up regardless. It's like life can just knock us over with a feather.

Somehow, even with the blindside, I know that "why me?" is the wrong question. There was no getting off of this rollercoaster ride while it was in full swing. So, the more I thought about it, why not me? As my coach reiterated over and over and over again, the world has cancer. We all have cancer cells. I don't know if that's true or not but it helped me to think, *Why not me?* This felt like a better question. I certainly would not want anyone else to be the one carrying the cancer. I decided I would carry it. I would fight. I would breathe into every itty bitty, microscopic cancer cell and take it on. Let's go! You want to fight? I'm going to kick your dis-eased ass now, okay? Yes, and, cross my fingers, and hope not to die.

did fight. And I was not the 95 percent who had stage 1 cancer. Who knows how long I was sick before they caught it? Who knows why I had cancer or why I'm still here. Here's what I know: I *am* still here. I will tell you I am not okay with the fact that I had cancer but I am at peace with it. Because I did have cancer. I had cancer like I have blue eyes. I couldn't control it. No one in my family history had ever had melanoma. My family has a much higher rate of heart disease in women than anything else, and addictions. But not cancer. I was the one. Just like I was the one who was shorter than the rest of the women in the family. I said earlier that I don't believe in luck, and I don't. I believe in life. It's not a test; it's life. And I believe that healing is possible.

And I will admit to you, on my knees, I do not understand why I have survived much of what I survived. It's not luck, I'm certain of that, but I don't know what it is if it's not luck. I choose to believe it's a commitment to life and choosing to come back to life, over and over again. And as Byron Katie says, "It's God's Business." *A Course in Miracles* says, "Nothing real can be threatened, nothing unreal exists." I focused on that during this time because I knew that whether I lived or died from cancer wouldn't be up to me. It was bigger than me. I could only commit to life as my best. The sooner that we stop trying desperately to question or figure it all out the more life we will give ourselves access to living. We are alive, until we aren't. What is real for me is that my body is phenomenal and has always carried me through. My body has stood for my strength, even when I refused to. My body kept me and my babies alive and continues to keep me alive. What I knew for sure when cancer arrived is that I would not be a statistic. Fuck statistics.

And then statistics blindsided me again. Upon initial diagnosis, I was told, for sure, "You're going to be okay. You have a 95 percent chance that we got all of the cancer in the initial surgery." The initial surgery happened while I was still seven months pregnant. The tumor was on my left arm and they cut down to the bone from my shoulder to my elbow and took wide margins of flesh and tissue, as much as they could. That was all they could do until the baby inside of me was safely born. The doctors said that the tissue that they took out looked healthy. They couldn't "stage" the cancer (tell what stage, 1 to 4, the cancer was) until the baby was born because it required that I be injected with radioactive dye. This meant an early C-section at thirty-eight weeks to protect both me and the baby. We waited for almost three long months. I was already very pregnant and now add to that the emotional weight of the terror of a cancer diagnosis and nothing else could be done until the baby was born. My worst nightmare. There's nothing to do. I can only pray, take good care of me and my body for the baby and wait. Once the baby was born, the placenta was clear meaning there was no cancer in the placenta. The baby girl was healthy and going to be okay. It was like my feet just hit the dock again after crossing Lake Ontario with my father during a storm. But before I knew it, it was on to the next surgery to stage the cancer.

Driving three-and-a-half hours to the cancer hospital three weeks post-partum with a newborn was torture. Every minute in the car felt like hours. My husband held steady as he drove and his strength and kind, loving eyes grounded and comforted me. But he was scared, too; it was undeniable that he was having his own nightmarish experience that neither of us could just wake up from. And then there was my oldest daughter's eyes full of fear and horror. I couldn't tell her it was all going to be okay. I couldn't love us all enough to get us to the other side of this. I couldn't change or stop cancer. There are no words to describe the immense terror I felt. Pulling up to the hospital was horrifying. It was like a cancer city. So unfair. So many people crying. So many people dying. None of them asked to be there and yet, here we all were with a piano player in the lobby and volunteers passing out graham crackers as we waited to see the professionals who held our lives in their hands.

Walking through the doors on cancer staging surgery day, I knew, that life just took on a whole new meaning and my life, obviously, was never going to be the same again. Now that the baby was delivered, the surgeons could take out a few lymph nodes as a precautionary measure, just to make sure that the cancer hadn't spread. They injected the radioactive, lifesaving dye (talk about an oxymoron) into my arm to see which lymph node the dye drained into. Three lit up like a Christmas tree and were removed immediately. They said that the lymph nodes looked healthy and were sent off to pathology. Then we waited—again.

And then there was the phone call days later that had my legs give out. It was all happening so fast and I was dizzy with fear. I will never forget that phone call. I knew it was bad when my doctor, the surgeon himself, called me personally to tell me that the cancer had in fact spread. I was among the 5 percent. He was shocked, he said. The statistics were not always accurate. He was so sorry. I could barely hear him. Then I hung up. I couldn't breathe. I couldn't see or hear. It was like all of my senses gave out in that chunk of time that lasted between when I answered the phone and when I had the strength to speak. I remember calling my mom, calmly telling her she needed to come over. The craziest piece of this double blindside was that now statistically I was pretty much fucked. My body was most likely not going to make it. There was a treatment, but it only added a less than 10 percent chance that I would live. When I asked my oncologist if that slim percentage was really worth it he said, "Well do you want to die? It's this or you die." So cold. So matter-of-fact. I couldn't let myself go there, down the "I am probably going to die" drain. I became a machine. I literally became a machine and stepped into Rebeccah 12.0. I felt so alone but I turned the volume all the way up on my commitment to life and decided that statistics were overrated.

That was when I decided to start listening to and aligning with my body. People were so kind, mostly, once they found out that I was as sick as I was. I remember deciding that I had to talk about it. Get the truth out, Rebeccah. Don't keep it in. People will feel your energy and they will know that something is wrong. What I knew is that I would never know why cancer was in my body. I'm pretty sure that "why" is the most absurd and ridiculous question ever asked. And many have asked me, "Why do you think you got cancer?" Who would I choose to be now and how would I choose to live now, in my world anyway, are better questions. I started talking on the radio, on social media. I didn't care who listened. I just knew my job was to give my truth a voice because anything else was me reinforcing and creating a cancerous environment for my body, my family, and my life.

Facebook became a journal and my way of communicating. I received a lot of judgement for that. It was too hard to have to share the updates one on one, so I posted. I posted and I got feedback. Everyone had an opinion: Don't share so much. Thank you for sharing. Why are you sharing? The list goes on. My only comfort was in getting and being as real as I could be. I knew that I had nothing to hide. I knew I had nothing to lose, so I wrote.

I had a three-week-old baby, a gorgeous ten-year-old at home, my dream husband and business, and now this was really, *really,* serious. Let the surgeries begin. Let the reality checks come. Bring on the chemo, because it's the only treatment available and I certainly don't want to die. This was my journey and story. Now it was a whole new game. This was a brand-new episode of Oprah that I hadn't planned on being the feature story for. It didn't matter what I wanted though; it was life, and the ultimate reality check that made me realize I was about to begin the journey of meeting myself. Who was I going to be now? It's easy to be your best and great when life goes our way, but what about when it all falls apart? I wasn't ready. I was afraid. But I was willing to fight for my life, and I did. It was easy to be the best of me when life was going well and every dream I'd ever had, had come true. Could I be the best of me in the face of cancer? I decided that I was going to be or die trying.

It was amazing the opinions, advice, calls, gifts, messages, and ghosting that occurred during cancer season. I got to see what was real about my life in a way that I had never been able to see clearly before, didn't see coming, and honestly wasn't prepared for. I had zero symptoms. That was the craziest part of all, for me anyway. I wasn't sick in a way where I *felt* sick. But I was so sick. I didn't feel sick though. Was this really happening? It was such a mindfuck. I decided quickly that I didn't care about statistics, I needed to let my body tell me what to do. No one else's opinion mattered. I created an army of support. Who I was back then was preparing for war. And because of cancer, my war with life ended. I learned that an entirely different experience of support was possible. That was the first and last army of support I created. "Thank you" will never be enough to all of the healers that I attracted. I had a yoga therapist, cranial sacral therapist, chiropractors, acupuncturist, coach, traditional oncologists both locally and hours away, massage therapists, and eventually personal trainers and physical therapists supporting me in fighting for my life. Aligning with my body suddenly seemed like such a good idea. I felt as if I had any chance at survival, I had better start talking to and listening to my body. What a concept! This was quite literally the opposite of how I had been living pre-cancer. It was what felt right then, though. I lit a match and burned the option of failure and dying from cancer like it was my new job, because it was.

Some people treated me as if I was going to die. I don't know where the voice inside of me came from that said, "Don't you dare treat me like I'm not going to survive this. If you talk to me like I am going to die or treat me like I'm going to die, or even look at me like I'm going to die, I will not be around you right now," is something that I said to more people than I can count. "If you can't see me as healthy and healing through this then I will not be around you right now.

Don't you dare plan my funeral. See me as alive and thriving. *Please*."

My soul sister Niki said to me once as I was about to go in for more testing, "All that is about to happen is, you are going in for testing, you will get through the tests and then you will get information." How right she was. She said to me, and I will never forget this conversation as long as I am alive, "You will get information and then you will decide what to do. And you will know what to do." What was so beautiful about this woman's strength and perspective to me was that she wasn't talking to a sick person who was dying. She was talking to her friend who still had her life ahead of her. I will never forget that phone call. I was so scared and yet the results were going to be the results. The results were not going to be about me. What I was going to do with the results was about me. Doing what it took to get through the tests so that I could get the results was about me. The show called my life wasn't over yet. It was all so much bigger than me.

What I would love for you to think about is, does life have to bring you to your knees and kick your ass in your worst nightmare format for you to start being all about how you are living your one life? Is it going to take a natural disaster or crisis for you to wake up to your power and life's ability to fight for you? Are you prepared to stop preparing for war? You are so much more powerful than you realize. The power in you is talking and does know what is best. Your power is on your side and can't hurt anyone. Powerlessness is what hurts people in all of its many flavors. Power is steadfast and relaxed with nothing to prove. What's it going to take for you to embrace how powerful you are? It doesn't have to be what I went through. Life doesn't have to get louder for you to step into listening more to your inner guidance system, which is where your power lives. If you are going to listen to anything, please believe that there is more power in you for you to step into. And if you are in crisis just please keep going. Know that you do have it in you to unearth the best of you now, because your life and the experience you have of your life depends on it.

What if we all can use every experience we find ourselves in exactly as it is, as an opportunity to love and honor ourselves, our lives, and each other more? What if we choose to use every set of perfect storm circumstances as a means to grow into our own greatness? And then we can fight from that perspective and as that perfectly equipped version of ourselves. We won't win if we fight and resist and panic and shut our power down instead of turning it up, stepping into "bring it" mode as the force to be reckoned with that we truly are. Life is happening and what you are facing now, what you are squaring off with that is in front of you is there and not going away. So lead. Powerfully. Choose to live through and lead through what's showing up as the version of you that you can be, that is required to win even in the face of what may seem like or feel like hell. What I know is that you have all the power you need to survive this moment, and the next, and the next in a way where you live through versus survive through the situation. What I want is for you to learn how to *do better* than survival. Not better than other people. Better for you than you have been doing. "Better than" survival means new and different and fully living. And that's available to you. Not available once life works itself out. It's available now. But you will have to be brave to get beyond survival into fully living. We think that new and different is scary. But isn't living powerless to our past and our present, scared, suffering, and just surviving, scarier?

I promise that it's okay for you to fall in love with you and your life. And it's possible. I'm not being optimistic or positive, I am whispering possibility in your ear. What will it take for you to start driving your life in the direction that you actually want to go, powerfully? You see it. I know you do. You want it. I know you do. You can taste it. I know you can. You are alive and gorgeous and it's time for you to turn the volume up on how powerful you really are. Why not you, to hope and create and dream? Why not you, to fail, get your heart broken, and want to quit but instead you don't? It's okay to want to quit, just don't. Why not you, to keep going when everyone else is giving up? Why not you to be the voice that instead of saying I can't, instead begins saying, I can find a way, like a prayer?

Why not you to be the one to get through the obstacle everyone said and you feared was impossible? It's like the sword in the stone. Someone gets to do and live your dream. Someone gets to survive your version of hell. Why not you? Why not now? We think we need more time. We don't need more time. What's possible is to use our voices and step up our commitment to living powerfully and free. I know it hurts. Where does it hurt? How long has it been hurting? It's time for emotional triage now; relief is coming but it's you that you have been waiting for. You already know how to live through pain. So what if they say it's impossible? (And oh, they will!) Move forward anyway.

It is this simple. And when it feels like your life is falling apart and no one gets it and there is no way to win, I'm asking you to remember that you have power that will carry you through. As long as you won't give up there is a way to win. Please trust that you are strong enough to keep moving forward even in the most hurtful and darkest corners of your mind and in your life. Life won't stop. The earth moves freely and fast. You will fall. You will fail. You will cry, scream, sweat, and bleed. It's all life and you are still here. I know it's brutal and some days your best will be to just keep breathing and you won't be able to get out of bed.

I was in bed for nine months after being diagnosed with cancer.

I couldn't walk because of nerve damage side effects from the chemotherapy I was on. I had a new baby and twelve surgeries and drop foot and it hurt. My God, did it hurt. Yet both my soul and body went through the most incredible healing during the most nightmarish year of my life. Surgeries piled on and my body never had time to recover. Then chemo had me so toxic that the nerves in my right leg began to die and my foot locked up and I had drop foot. I didn't even know what drop foot was before cancer. I didn't know that at thirty-four I could be pregnant and happy and have the life of my dreams one day and then BOOM, cancer. But it happened. These things happen to beautiful people who didn't ask for it every day, maybe even every minute of every day.

Who we choose to be in the face of anything is the question. Every nightmare eventually ends and we wake up. Same is true for difficult circumstances. What if where we really get to meet ourselves is inside of our very own past personal hell? That's the key: let it really be your past and no longer a part of life right now. We can find out who we are and what we're made of when we face that hell. And I think it's easier to face hell when we realize it's over, and that facing it really is what will change everything. To survive hell we've got to stand up tall, breathe, and lead, powerfully, becoming more than we've ever been because we got willing to face, move through, and conquer the emotions underneath the feelings like never before. Focus on the endgame, not the moment. And we can. *You can.* I could. I didn't know it at the time but I remember lying in bed, not even able to hold the new baby because I'd had so many surgeries on my arm, and wanting it to end. Then I decided that it wasn't too late to let my best be enough while I focused on getting well.

My family brought the baby to me and that had to be enough. I could touch her cheek and kiss her face. I could look into her then grey eyes and see both of our souls at the same time. I could pour love and light into her and simply love her. That was enough, it had to be. Until I could hold her, I got to see her. I got to hear her little noises and watch her sweet face recognizing mine. I got to stay married and loved and supported and be a mom and a woman who was stronger than she ever knew she could be. I showed up and chose to believe that I had what it took to kick cancer's ass. *Why not me?* Being capable of coming out the other side of this and coming back to life is what I kept telling myself. *Why not now?* Controversially (I am not recommending this to you) I quit chemo and listened to my body as it told me what I needed to survive. I played the game of cancer "all in" and didn't wish it away. That was the only way that I knew that I would make it. And by the grace of God I did. I know what it's like to be in the blackest dark not knowing if there will ever be light again. I do not believe that I cured cancer but I did choose to powerfully commit to living like I was going to live. Against the odds and statistics, my commitment to life and my army of support, including my coach, held. I knew I might die. But if cancer was going to take me out, I would die fighting. I would be the light in the cancer. And I was. For my girls. For my husband. For my future. What I know now was the war I was really fighting was the inner war within myself. Cancer is the last time I go to war. I did the best I could then, that was enough. And now I know better. No matter how dark it is or feels or you fear it's going to get, the light is you. The hope is you. The leader that is required to step forth and carry you is you. I'm not saying you are alone and have to do it alone. I am saying that you are the only one that can tame the dragons in your mind that want to breathe fire all over your hope and progress. You are the one to reckon with. No one can do it for you. It has to be you. It's *always* been you.

You can be free of resistance to what you have no control over knowing how powerful you are, no matter what, as you move forward in your life from this point on. Whatever hell you are in, or have been in, your power is carrying you and your body holds your power. It has the answers. It wants to help and it is definitely talking. I know it's been terrifying at times but life doesn't have to continue to be terrifying. You can end the war. You are still here. Have you ever had thoughts at some point about wanting someone to save you? They aren't coming. Look in the mirror at the hero in the room ready to carry you out of the flames and into your future. It's you! You are powerful. Now you have a choice to make. Will you choose to become a survivor?

We have seasons and we face storms. And we are still here. But we won't be here forever. How will you play your "right now"? How will you lead your "right now"? The world is watching. The world doesn't want you to fail. And the world hasn't met you in all of your power, yet. The world hasn't seen the possibility that you see. Go show the world that it's possible. It's time to live. Go for the gold. Go for the win. Go for the healing. Go for freedom.

It's so easy to think that we don't have what it takes. That thinking gives us permission to give up, which serves no one. And how does that feel? Terrible, right? Your right to live powerfully is here now. Nothing can threaten how powerful you are while you are still alive. You do have what it takes to beat the odds—if you will step fully into your power. It's your time to create a life that speaks to you on a soul level.

I know it's hard at times to imagine that the critics really don't matter. I know it can be easier to listen to the one person who criticizes you instead of multiple people that may be cheering you on at the same time. It's time to think for yourself. Decide for yourself. Let the possibilities unfold.

I've worked in several school districts, and I do a powerful presentation on assertiveness with K through twelfth-graders. I begin by asking the students two questions. First, raise your hand if you think you are better than someone else. Then, raise your hand if you think someone else is better than you. All of the kindergartners raise their hands to at least one of those questions. It's so sad to me because whether they are the one who thought that they were better or the one who thought others are better, separation and powerlessness are already in motion. We're all here, alive, and living our lives, doing our best. It's time to stop our powerlessness and modeling powerlessness in its tracks instead of fighting for it. It's time to stop desperately trying to measure which end of the hierarchy we're on and let that ladder of lies come crashing down. Instead, the goal is to be the best of ourselves for the world, because we can.

One of the greatest games I ever wrote for a women's seminar, I called the defensiveness game. It's a good one. I had the women get in pairs and defend their dramas and their pain. I wanted the women to hear themselves fighting for their pain and their obstacles. It was fascinating to watch. The women got so heated and really committed to their struggles. What was so powerful about this exercise was that the women got to validate themselves instead of needing to be validated. But then they got to wake up to what they were validating and course correct.

Growing pains are real and once some light is shed on where our resistance lies, the truths that we've been living that contradict the real goal come out. The power in the obstacle starts to melt away. The moments we defend our powerlessness we won't get back. Whatever you are seeing take that information as good news and access to more powerful choices moving forward. Please don't use this as more ammunition against yourself. I don't want us beating ourselves up more, over lost time. That's not the point. We haven't lost time, in fact from this level of awareness we are giving ourselves so much time back. The point is, are you paying attention now? What happens from here? Are you going to continue to defend who you aren't or who you've been and be right about your pain and your stuck and continue to defend it? Or, will you at least consider stepping into new territory where you get to meet and experience even more of the power that is in you and that is you?

I understand. This is in the way and that is in the way. They won't understand or they won't stick around. You might get left. You might get laughed at. You might fail. Yes. Those things may happen. And you'll still be here, in your body, living your life, your way. We so badly want to meet our powerful selves and then we make sure that we aren't going to get to live powerfully. We lose so much power when we won't even try because of the peanut gallery. Let you and the voices in your head, at least just for today, be the voices that you stand up to. Don't concern yourself with the others, yet. Start with simply breathing into your power and let's see what happens.

THE WORLD DOESN'T KNOW ABOUT YOU YET

You are alive. Why not step into and own your greatness? Greatness is a big word. To me, living in to our greatness is the essence of fully living or "all in" living. There is no benefit, as far as I can tell, in holding our greatness back from the world. In my experience of working with hundreds of thousands of people in different capacities, I know that they are all coming for one thing. That thing is to connect to who they really are, and then to become the person that's brave enough to stand in the power of being their authentic self.

We can permanently break up with the part of ourselves that believes it's "right" to cower. For so long, I couldn't put into words the essence of how it felt to go "in" and "out" of being fully me. If I cower then I can't hear. And then I can't think. And then I'm not safe. And then I just want to hide and put myself under the covers and hold on until "it" ends. I can see how this coping skill and comfort measure kept me undermining myself and what I stand for. Can you see this for you as well?

So many times I froze or ran or resisted instead of bravely and powerfully leading. Those moments have collateral damage. I'm sorry to anyone I've negatively impacted when all I knew how to do was to freeze, run, or resist. I can't change those moments but I can and have learned from them. When we know better we have a responsibility to do better. And our best at the time was enough and now let's move forward. Let's be all of ourselves so that we can be more careful with people. We can't be a loose cannon and expect to be respected or of any type of real service. Cancer had me officially break up with cowering and with being at war with myself and my life. Will you join me? I am great and so are you. I don't know why it's so painful to stand in that but I do know it's true for all of us. It's more selfish for us to play small and scared as we run away from our power than it's ever been to be our full-on best. Greatness to me means commitment to being all in with ourselves. Only from that place can we truly commit to people. And if you are thinking that this doesn't apply to you, if you suffer at all, you are not owning your power yet. Suffering comes from fear which means that fear has taken over your brain. When fear takes over, we are powerless. Note that powerlessness can look like aggression; it doesn't always look passive or submissive. What is your favorite way to be powerless? Do you prefer to freeze, fight, run away, something else? Situations, circumstances, people, and external factors can be slippery and subtle but just know that they are never, ever, more powerful than you are.

Every morning, I wake up clear as the cloudless sky that there is nothing more powerful in my life than my body, mind, and soul. Nothing can take me out while I am still here. Nothing can take you out while you are still here. I'm asking you to break up with the part of you that's been clinging to survival mode for so long. You do not need approval, reassurance, or permission. Thank you to all of the teachers in my life that have supported me in getting brave and strong enough to withstand the fear-based storms of being my fully *authentic self*. Those two words are small and yet mean everything. Service is my life purpose. Leading in possibility is my life purpose. That's all I want to do. I love being alive and I love people. It's so much fun even in the darkest and most difficult moments for me. I want to see and find my weak spots. I encourage you to try this on, too. We do not have to make up for being here on the planet. I want us to be who we really are. I know that the only solution is to be all of ourselves, with an open heart, caring about each other.

Many live in the dark rather than the light. It's suffocating to keep ourselves small and far away from all of what life has to offer us. Childhood demons, traumas, and heartbreaks are the only real walls we've all found ourselves up against. Every wall is the past on repeat disguised as something new. It got painful to be fully real and transparent; then we turned the volume down on our passion and our light faded. Be the brightest bulb ever turned on! It's your only job. The dark is real and it's coming but it's not coming for you or from you. The dark is just there. It's not your fault or even about you at all. The darkness is real. *So is the light.*

Stop denying the dark while you allow the light in you to give you access to your next right step and you are free. Admit where you find comfort and solace in the dark and know there's life outside of that small, limited, and often painful way of living. There is nothing wrong with you, even when you are hiding in the darkest corners of your soul. You just don't have to live there. You are free to be light, and to seek and step into the light is your right. You could choose now. You could choose to step into a "Bring it on!" attitude. You could choose to love and be and experience all of you. Let the world watch. Let the world eat its heart out. Go into the place in you that knows who you really are. It's not about finding yourself. It's about choosing who you want to be and then becoming that powerful version of yourself. Breathe into that place. If you don't think that you can find it, just keep looking. Commit to finding *you*. It won't happen overnight, but you being light and free is a beautiful gift that only you can give yourself and all of us.

Like a great detective you'll find evidence to support why the world won't be able to handle your power. Explore those triggers so that you can be free of them. Our triggers keep us powerless. Avoiding conflict keeps us powerless. My coach has said to me in some of my most painful triggers and upsets, "Nothing is happening, Rebeccah. Nothing at this moment is happening." What I took away from that was a new question that I could ask myself, "What's going on with you, in you?" That's such a great question and how I experience all upsets now. We are frozen in the past and running away from, instead of toward, our futures when we are willing to shut our souls off or turn the volume down on being all of who we are. Nothing can take you down. Nothing can break you down. Life is just showing you where you won't stand in being fully you, yet. Why not bravely step into your lightest life? There is a way back home to yourself. There is no benefit in living small or compartmentalizing your life. You are more powerful than both the darkness and the dawn and dawn is always coming.

How many nights have you spent crying yourself to sleep, wanting more? I spent so many years missing that my heart was still beating not realizing how powerful I was. Do you miss you? If so, you have just had temporary amnesia and forgot who you are. For years I spent night after night crying myself to sleep. I would cry so hard that I couldn't breathe. Most of the time I felt like I was going insane, really. Sometimes I would think to myself that going crazy might be easier than feeling how painful my life felt. What I didn't realize was that my soul, life and body were waiting for me to reconnect to myself. Your life is one you can keep close and nurture. Your power holds a place for you in your life and in the world. Your heartbeat keeps the beat of your life. Cry yourself to sleep whenever it's needed and know that with each tear you are shedding the pain of being who you are not instead of being who you are. Also know that the pain can be moved through and forgiven. It's time to stop looking for reasons to cry yourself to sleep as you wait for your life to begin. It's time to live and to look forward to your life. Will you stand up or stay down? It's up to you, beautiful soul.

Life is moving with or without you. Your feet move, too, but in what direction? Are you moving in the right direction, for you? You don't have to step into your personal power, but you can. There are plenty of obstacles, I know. But it's your life and it's your call how quickly and in what direction you will move your feet. Toward the light? Toward the dark? Farther from you? Closer to you?

THE CANCER

I feel like a whale. My body hurts. I don't know anything other than I have malignant cancer and they can't stage the cancer until the baby is out. I'm driving down the road crying and yelling in my car, insanely irate. I feel like my body has betrayed me, again. I don't know if I will live or die or if the baby is okay. And then it hit me as fast as the wind can carry away a letter that gets dropped: I am alive and my body isn't just keeping me alive but the baby is alive too. I feel her kicking me as if to say, "Hey, calm down Mom. I'm still here. Can't wait to meet you!" I decide to focus on knowing that I will meet the baby and that we will make it. My tears change form and gratitude, genuine gratitude which had been a stranger to me until that very moment, washes my face and melts the fear around my heart. Maybe I am more powerful than I knew? Maybe my body is more powerful than I've ever given it credit for being.

We made it. I needed a goal that I could be all in with as long as I was still breathing. The goal was life. I had cancer. I quit chemo. And then I realized I might actually survive. I never anticipated how devastating it would feel to understand that life was never going to be the same again. It was a whole new layer of feeling like it wasn't fair. And it wasn't fair. My business, marriage, body, relationships, my life would never go back to the way they were. We all are still reeling from a global pandemic that taught us this very lesson. So when I started to see the possibility of me getting well, I got depressed. Then my phenomenal coach asked me, "Now what? What fits in with you now? Who will you be now?" She said, "Your job is not to find a way to fit into the world. Your job now is to create a life that fits in with you." I'll be honest, I was terrified and a little pissed that she wasn't feeling sorrier for me. I wanted to feel sorry for myself, at first. But I also wanted something to look forward to and I had zero interest in cancer winning or defining me. Her words soothed my fears like aloe on a sunburn and gave me hope that I could in fact powerfully create a life that fit in with me now.

Your dreams are only as accessible to you as your willingness to be the person it takes to move into the direction toward them, regardless of obstacles. Get it. Get up. You get to hope. You get to embrace how powerful you really are. The key is to understand that nothing ever needed to be different. You stepping into your power regardless of circumstance is the new name of the game. Nothing outside of you is more powerful than you. You can identify as unshakably whole if you will be brave and powerful, trusting yourself and your good intentions. The world will do what it does and that no longer has to determine how powerful or not you feel.

Journal EXERCISE

- When did you feel the most powerful?

- If you were no longer asking "Why me" or waiting for permission, how would your life change?

- Journal about the worst-case scenarios of you being all of you and taking a "Why not me?" approach to life.

- Journal about the support you would need to face these worst-case scenarios.

- What would life feel like if you were living fully in your power?

- If you were being the most powerful version of yourself, how would you be living? What would stay the same? What would need to change? What would you choose to pursue?

- What does the most powerful version of you want to do with your life?

Chapter Seven

THE PURPOSE

The purpose of living is to get the most
out of your life.

I am with this man but he does not want to be with me. And
I have a young daughter. We moved to Las Vegas, together,
where I don't want to be. My family is on the opposite end
of the country. Single mom life is not fabulous and neither is
Las Vegas. The guy is fun and attractive, most days, but deep in
my heart I do not want to be where I live and I don't want to live
how I'm living. I am tolerating. I am settling. I'm dumbing it down
because I don't want to be alone. I long to know I am worth loving.
But I don't love myself. I am living a life of trying to fit in, desperate to be
worthy. I make up that the most important thing is whether or not my boyfriend wants me instead of being brave enough to admit that I'm unhappy
too. I want a fairy tale. I want someone to want to raise my daughter with
me. I want to start over and get married and do it better than I did the first
time. One night I have a dream that the man I'm with at the time is crying

and apologizing for not wanting to marry me or have a future with me. This is my biggest fear—not being enough, again. And then he says to me, "It's like I have my dream woman but I can't reach you. It's like you are behind the glass." This is music to my ears. I can do better. I can learn how to put my walls down and maybe then he will want me and love me. But I'm scared. What if I do even more work to grow and he still doesn't want me?

And then I have a phone call with a friend. That friend spoke gospel and I hung on his every word. He says to me, "Rebeccah, you are with a safe man who loves you. The worst thing that can happen is that you learn how to put your walls down, let love in, and it doesn't work out. If you break up before you do this work you are still going to have to learn how to put your walls down with a new person. Do everything you can to grow and heal with this partner or your patterns will repeat." I listened. My purpose changed from being needy for validation, love, and security from this man, to becoming solid within myself with an open heart.

I did the work. It wasn't the right relationship. I was crushed but I had learned what intimacy was. I learned I could survive another heartbreak and the trauma of being so certain that I had to have a man love me for *me* to know I was enough. I left Las Vegas with two dogs, my daughter, and no clue where I would end up, where we would live, or what would be next. It was the beginning of me learning how to stand on my own two feet leading my life, my way.

BE THE SOURCE OF YOUR OWN ENCOURAGEMENT

Encouragement means your courage game is strong enough to believe you can do it. Being the source of your own encouragement means that you are able to talk to and love yourself in such a way that you are the one validating, believing in, and encouraging yourself. How do you beat fear, guilt, and regret so that you can find your purpose? How do you heal the thing you think you can't heal? How do you defeat quitting on yourself? How do you learn how to listen and connect more to yourself and others? How do you have deeper and more emotional intimacy in your relationships? It's all the same answer. Become the source of your own encouragement. In my work with clients, even in conversations with family and friends, what I see as a theme is people wanting anything outside of themselves to become their lifeline. This has been true for me as well. For years, I sought the people I thought had the answers. Courage to me is about embodying a willingness to face, move through, and conquer fear. It's also about knowing that guidance is out there but the answers are in you. I'll say it one more time: to me, courage is about willingness to face, move through, and conquer fear so that you can find your way and your next right answer. And the only one who can do that for me is me. And the only one who can do that for you is you. That's what it means to become the source of your own encouragement.

I see it almost every single day, where I'm interacting with a gorgeous soul that will do anything but become the source of their own encouragement. And this has been a really hard lesson for me—realizing that courage is always there, within. Sure, it can seem so much easier to believe in and buy into the fear and the doubt, and to be unwilling to face, move through, or conquer fear. But when you recognize that courage is already there and you just haven't known how to tap into it, you can hope again. When you get willing to stop dancing around your only issue, which is you won't be the source of your own encouragement, you get closer to your purpose and more free. I know that's a bold statement, but think about it, your only real problem is that you aren't the source of your own encouragement. What if the only issue I have ever had has been that Iwouldn't stand up for and validate myself?

I'm not asking you to be an egomaniac or arrogant. I'm saying you have it in you to be your own guide, to be your own center of your own life. But we think other people are smarter, sexier, funnier, more qualified, and more talented. But none of that's true when it comes to you and your life. None of that's true when it comes to knowing who you are, knowing what you want, knowing how you feel, and knowing what you need. I'm asking you to get really honest. And when I'm talking about being the source of your own encouragement, I'm not suggesting that you go at life alone. I am just suggesting this: it's about time for you to become your own lifeline. I used to have almost an addiction to finding the next answer for my next step from other people, but following another person's map never really worked out. I needed to learn how to create my own road map through learning from them and through learning what wasn't working for me, so that I could find what would work for me.

What if today you let yourself plant the seed within you to be your own encourager and let that become your lifeline? Nurture that seed and make this your only purpose. Your purpose is to get the most out of your life by learning how to connect to and follow your internal guidance system while being the source of your own encouragement. Not easy but it's possible. How would life be different if every single solution was in you? I think it is. If the answers were in you, if the light in you was the only guidance you needed, and then you could see the right choice, the right support, the right path, the right people to collaborate with, for you, from a different energy and vibration. *There isn't a right way or a wrong way to live your life. Life can get much clearer. There is only what works for you.*

Earlier in this book we talked about old bad habits. Now I'm going to declare that there really are no bad habits either. There is only what works and what doesn't, when it comes to living how you want to live and feeling how you want to feel. How would life feel if you no longer depended on other people to encourage, validate, and "get" you? The energy of needing other people's perceptions to carry you through keeps you needy and powerless, forgetting how badass and powerful you are. I'm inviting you to try on a new energy of, "We're in this together, shoulder to shoulder, supporting each other as each one of us is the source of our own encouragement and our own lifelines."

When you make your purpose about becoming the source of your own encouragement, then you model that possibility for every life in front of you. It's an honor to support you in your healing. Now is the time for you to become a source of your own encouragement and your own lifeline. Make this day, this month, this time, the moment when you take leadership of your own life.

NEXT-LEVEL LIVING: READY WHEN YOU ARE

Let's talk on a deeper level about goals. How many times have you not followed through on your goals? How many times have you started and stopped and didn't know how to restart or finish? I've got a few reasons for you that I hope resonate. The first reason is because your goal may have been built on a foundation of shame, or believing that you should be further along than you are. Or maybe you believe that something is wrong with you for not being where you think you should be. Another reason could be that you were trying to prove something to yourself or other people and that could mean pursuing goals that aren't really what you actually want for your life. Finally, you may have been using your goal to try to find validation from external sources, in an attempt to fill yourself up. What I love about dreams and goals is that they offer us an opportunity to commit.

Here's some more soul food to chew on. What if thinking about choosing a goal or a dream feels like pressure? Here's what I suggest you try on instead of worrying about what that next goal or dream is: *focus on what you want.* If you already believe that you can become the source of your own encouragement, the next step is to get clear on what your "big want" is. You get to choose, right? Who are you going to be next? What do you want next? What if that is all that matters? Start with asking yourself those questions. Looking back at times when I made my goals and dreams come true, I realize that I went *all in,* in being the person it took to create them. *Because I wanted it.* I was unwilling not to win and to get all the way there. I came from a place of inspiration and excitement instead of fear. Anytime I've made a new dream a reality, including the Healing IS Possible mission and movement which includes this book, I wanted it more than I was afraid it wouldn't work out.

What I want for you, what I want for me, what I want for all of us is for us to commit to being the person it takes because we're inspired and excited about the next result we want to create in our lives. Just pick, pick one thing at a time and decide that you are *it,* you are the hero. You are your own fairy godmother! And it's okay to risk bravely and courageously letting the world watch you stumble and fall and scuff up your knees on your way to where you want to get. It's okay to let them watch. You don't need a new year's resolution or even a goal if that word doesn't resonate. Commit to the life you want. If this calls to you, all you have to do is pick one "want" at a time to get your life more and more looking and feeling the way you've always wanted it to go. Take one dream at a time that you want more than anything else to manifest. That gets you your life, the way you want it—regardless of how it's been, regardless of what you've seen, regardless of the difficulties right now. All it takes is true commitment. This is your purpose; or at least it could be. Anyone who looks at a dream like, "Yeah, there's no way, I'm not going to get this," won't get there. Period.

What if what you want isn't that far away? Maybe it's right in front of you. Choosing to believe that you are closer than you think automatically gets you there faster. It's a choice. It can be a decision that now this is the next result I want, whatever word, goal, dream, want, result, or commitment resonates with you. This is your time. This is your life. It's your right to get what you want. And if you're still breathing, you have what it takes to tap into your courage to create a result that surprises you, that you've dreamed about. And if you're someone that doesn't think that, you know what you want, I want to talk to you next, because here's what I'm going to suggest.

Here's a secret. Commitment can't trap you. You get to change your mind. It may be scarier to be close to "it," whatever your thing is. Don't be afraid to let yourself have and know that when you are ready for *more* and next, you get to have and create that for yourself too. And when the dead ends show up, pivot and keep going. It just wasn't that person, like my Mr. Las Vegas or the right job for you now. The Las Vegas relationship ending didn't mean I didn't get to have the marriage and family that I was dreaming of. When it doesn't work out or is no longer working, that just means it's time to reinvent. You do know what you want. Now be brave enough to risk, letting people see you going for it. If you know what you do not want, I guarantee you have it in you to dream up your next big, want, for yourself. And it can be trial and error. You know, I've wanted things that when I got them, I thought, *Oh, that wasn't as exciting as I thought it would be.* Maybe you can relate. But I still was the person that created it. I've run marathons. I did that one, three times, that was enough. You deserve to get what you want. What would life be like if you just decided, "I get what I want. I get what I want. I get what I want"? I want you to get what you want. It doesn't always come easily and there will be obstacles. But in the face of obstacles, I just want us to turn up the volume on our commitment, not going, *Oh, maybe I shouldn't go for it because there was an obstacle.* Every time you think, *Maybe this is a sign that I shouldn't actually pursue this thing,* remember: it's just a test of your commitment.

Start with just one. Just one goal that you are all in with. Make it a game. Play it like you can't lose. Play it like your life depends on it—because the life you want does. Once you burn the option of not making it you are left with only the option of success or die trying. For me, this feels more fun, more free. If there's a goal that you know you aren't all in with, so what? Pick another one. One goal at a time. Instead of thinking about what you *should* do, find what excites and inspires you the most. What's the point of living if we aren't going to get what we really want? The world can handle you happy, believe me. If the world can handle you half-assing your life and being miserable at times, it can handle you living as big, as loud, and as vibrant as you choose to be.

Do you love dogs? I do. Want to know what my first *all-in* commitment was? It was a dog. Her name was Kayla. She was beautiful. The red in her face, the lashes on her eyes, the blackest fur you've ever seen, carrying the kindest soul that I had ever been blessed to know. I rescued Kayla from a shelter and I just knew I'd be her person.

Nothing would have me ever not be there for that dog. I used to joke that she was the first thing that I had ever committed to on purpose. I really meant it when I adopted her. She was a nightmare for the first couple of years. One time I brought her to the nursing home I was working at and a lovely resident took her leash to pet her and Kayla ran her down the hall in her wheelchair. The woman said it was the most fun she had had in twenty years, but I was mortified! Kayla ate shoes, ran away more times than I can count, and cried out for love seeking negative attention more than I would have liked, but I was all in. Once I ran through a blizzard to get her and bring her home. She lived to be fifteen and we moved at least ten times together, all in, in our love for each other. When she started dying it was right after I quit chemo. It was as if she was telling me, I'm going now because you, the girls, and Mark (my husband) are all going to be okay. Find your all-in commitment. It's in you. You've earned it. You deserve it.

All in or all out. We can't be both places at the same time. I like to think of life as abundant and generous. I also like to think that I am constantly trading up when it's time for fresh and new. This doesn't mean that what I had wasn't precious, of course it was. It just means that there is a new beginning and I'm committed to forward motion and never feeling like I am going backwards. Sometimes though, even the backwards feels like progress to me. Why? Because I know with every breakdown it's time to grow to create fresh and new. Plus, I've learned what *doesn't* work for me.

What do you want to get out of your life? I'm asking you to have a vision for the life and future that you want to live so that you can fully experience the life that you have. If you can't see it, you can't create it. If you can only see how you think life "should be," that feels heavy and terrible. The more tenderly and patiently you love yourself into finding your own answers, the more your intuition will talk. Watch out for thinking that you don't have what it takes or that you can't. Instead of worrying about "Can I?" or "Can't I?" ask yourself "Will I?" or "Won't I?" Pursue your bliss and your fantasy life because it's yours for the taking.

What do you fantasize about when you daydream? What is your wildest dream for your life experience? What do you know you want but aren't moving your feet toward? You know why you think you can't, I'm certain of it. But what if you're wrong? What if you can and now all that's left is full-on commitment?

YOUR LIFE, YOUR KINGDOM

The process of going all in requires that everything that gets in the way of our commitment to fall out of the way. When your old life starts to unravel as you make way for your new life, it can feel scary. It may even feel like we're being punished or that we aren't supposed to want more or get more. You can choose to believe these things. Or, the closer you get and the worse it feels, you can recognize that you are that much closer to the finish line and it can feel fun and joyful, you just didn't know that before. Every time we're tempted to reject what's possible for us, we need to face the situation head-on to truly learn how to come fully alive. There is so much evidence to say that we can't. Who do we think we are? Why should we? I'm here as the megaphone of possibility saying: "Quit listening to any of the people, including the voice in your own brilliant mind, cautioning you against winning at your dreams! Seriously? The pro football player isn't saying, 'I might fumble so I shouldn't try.'"

The most romantic thing my husband ever said to me was that he can't turn the volume up on how much he loves me. I got mad at him post baby and cancer and threw it in his face that even cancer didn't make him more careful, gentle, or loving with me. He looked me right in the eye and said, "Do you think that cancer could change how much I love you? The volume was already turned all the way up on how much I love you. Cancer didn't change that." I was gobsmacked—and grateful. People want to lean out of the pain, the disillusionment when they decide, Oh, maybe this wasn't what I thought. We have to lean into what we can't stand to feel in order to get through to the other side of the pain.

What's the difference between those who commit and those who won't? Maybe just stuck fear. Maybe the non-committers just can't see the forest through the trees, yet. Maybe they are waiting for it to get so loud and painful they have to move. What if what we are waiting for is ourselves? You hold the key to every single thing you've ever wanted. Start listening. Start breathing into the pain and fear and uncertainty. You can be certain that if you stop moving you'll get nowhere. You can be certain that you get to choose in or out, of feeling what you don't want to feel. But you have to feel to move forward. All in is willingness. It doesn't mean you want to feel the pain or that you caused it. Healing means it doesn't hurt anymore. Address the pain that is real until it no longer hurts, believing that you can get to the place where nothing hurts. Decide that you are, ready or not, going to move through it to get what's meant for you on the other side of resistance bubbling up. Inspiration, freedom, and joy are waiting for you. Are you going to take what's your God-given right? Or keep waiting? All in is the answer, every time. Commitment doesn't have to mean that you have to do what you don't want to do, it's the exact opposite. Commit to what's right for you, it's enough. I gave up "doing the right thing" if it wasn't good for me and have honestly never felt

better. You can do this, too. In fact, I dare you to only commit to what
you want that takes care of and honors you and the life you want now,
from this moment forward. Every action. Every choice.

People are judging you already, based on their own filters, beliefs,
and programming that has nothing to do with you. So fear of being
judged as your excuse to not come back to life is silly. Do you want
to be judged for waiting or for creating? You choose. Art makes no
sense in the beginning and then it comes together, just like life. It's
messy to live free but it's more fun. I don't know about you, but I like
to have fun.

What if nothing is wrong? What if your life is always getting it
right? What if homeostasis is happening and it's all coming together?
How could that be, you may ask, when it hurts so much? If we let go of
control and get committed to living instead, we don't know what we
will be left with. Someday can be right now. Putting your life on hold
can be the old way, the way that you used to live. Those days can be
history starting today. What would life be like if you stopped giving
yourself permission to let self-doubt win?

If there are days or moments that knock the wind out of you,
even once you've committed, just stay in the game. If you want to
numb out, shut down, or run away, again, don't. Keep going while you
feel through your emotions. Because now you are more aware. The
next time an *I don't know if I can handle this* moment happens, ask
yourself, *Who am I going to be now while I acknowledge that I want to
run?* We don't need to be right or get our way; we need to know we
went for it. We've believed in our limitations more than believing in
and betting on ourselves and this is tragic. Please stop defending your
limitations and your obstacles. If you are in defensiveness mode you
stay stuck and maybe even get sick. Your greatness is on the other side

of your fear and your defensiveness. It really is. It's time to grow into your greatness. Bet on yourself. I'm betting on you.

But what does growing into your greatness even mean? If I'm taking a break to watch Netflix, does that mean I'm not great? If I want to enjoy a KitKat bar, does that not make me great? Needing a nap can be a great way to reset but so many people think that's lazy. For most of my twenties I went back and forth between over-exercising (without proper nutrition), crash dieting, anorexia and bulimia. For me, this looked like mostly food restriction and purging what I did eat. Ironically, for many years I considered my twenties the decade where I had my body "handled." I was a size 2 when I had mostly been more like an 8 or 10 in my teens and in college. What's interesting to me looking back now is how much value I placed on the numbers, my size and weight. I had numbers as the goal and really didn't care how I got to the right number, as long as I got there. How many days did I spend throwing up into a toilet? How many meals have I skipped fighting through hunger and weakness, white-knuckling my way from one task to the next, pushing my body to maximum capacity? What was the benefit? Of course there was a benefit—though some of you reading this might think there was no benefit. Let me explain.

The benefit to our choices drives why we do what we do. We don't do anything in life that doesn't have some sort of benefit or value associated with it. We do what's most valuable, in that moment period. We work for a paycheck. This is a hard topic because we think we know better. But we really don't know better than what we are doing, while we are doing it. We do what we know and there is comfort in that. Sometimes comfort is the benefit. We get something out of every choice that we ever make. When we're striving for greatness it's because there is a benefit. When we go against our greatness, it's also because of a benefit. The benefit is what allows rationalization and justification. It's also what can keep us stuck.

Stuck isn't all bad. We hear people say all the time, "The right time will come." I believe that's true. I also believe we can *opt out* of any behavior that keeps us further from our goals, especially body and health goals. Instead, we can make new choices that will actually get us closer to the finish line; you know, the one that on a soul level we really want to cross. We usually stop because of a stuck emotion that we don't want to feel. You can go further than you think you can go emotionally. We want to feel better but we don't want to feel. *You've got to be willing to feel to heal.* Feel through your anger, sadness, and fear to access your joy, ability to love, and your excitement again. We've all been crippled by fear at times, but emotions are not the enemy. They are your superpower! You get to get the pain out. Greatness, for me, is about knowing I went as far as I could, and then didn't stop there. I keep going just a little bit further, and just a little bit further. Autopilot is optional. Stopping and quitting is optional; so just don't.

Society romanticizes with emphasis that it's okay and normal to want to be anybody other than ourselves. Talk about a perfect way to keep your life in a perpetual state of panic and upset! Greatness comes from tapping into the part of you that knows what you do and do not want. Selfish? Sure. And what else is there other than living in alignment with yourself so that you can be as real and great as you can be with others? When you are "off" with yourself, people can feel it. When you aren't you, life feels off and relationships suffer. Again, that body knows. Use it. Listen to it. Trust and honor it. I promise that listening to and honoring your body will only allow you to thrive and feel how you want to feel. Listen more. Do less. Measure your worth with how connected to YOU, you are. Not how much others are approving.

Greatness requires us to go farther than we've been before. You can choose to enhance your life and your experience of life. We can reach for that next level which requires some serious stretching and commitment. Or, we can reach for the smaller, more comfortable and seemingly easier level, which requires selling out. We get to choose. We've all faced challenges and moments in life where we betrayed ourselves or sold out. Find me one person who hasn't been a sell-out somewhere. Greatness to me is giving up selling out. Being the person it takes to reach and stretch and grow. Some people might say, "Why should I? Life is good." Or, "I don't want to mess up what I have." All valid concerns and they are also concerns that will keep you a prisoner of your own life, while you sell you out.

When I was on my knees on the floor in the gas station bathroom, I was unwilling to be great. I was committed to feeling lost, trapped, and unwanted. How was this beneficial? I got to be right about how alone I was. I got to be right about how wronged I was. I got to be right about my mistrust of my body; it wouldn't even throw up for me. I knew that this was not how I wanted to live my life yet it was how I was living my life. I was committed to suffering and self-loathing. Have you been there? Can you relate? I was hating myself and my life and blaming myself for my circumstances. Have you been there? Can you relate? I let my knees hit the floor and bowed into a filthy toilet bowl praying for relief and for a miracle. What I couldn't wrap my head around at that time was that I was the miracle. I had to get up, off my knees, and bow into possibility and my future. I was surrendering into my fear and in essence giving up on my life. This meant that I was also giving up on my kid. I thought my problem was that I couldn't get thin enough, but my problem was that I wouldn't free myself from my past or my pain. Ironically, this time of my life I thought to myself, *Well, at least my body is handled.* I was so thin at 110 pounds. But my body was being tortured day after day, year after year. The torture was my normal. Belief in miracles didn't come until later.

Today, I believe in miracles and I think that the human body and its capacity to heal is one of life's greatest miracles. It's been liberating to surrender into the power and greatness of my body. For me it took cancer and a new baby and my oldest child and the man of my dreams that I was unwilling to give up on, to see that my body was a miracle. I had stage 3 cancer. I had a body that kept both the baby and me alive. I got to see my oldest get elected school president. I get to watch my youngest learn how to read. I get to watch my girls laugh and cry, dance and sing. I was there for my oldest daughter's first heartbreaking breakup with a boyfriend that she thought was her first real love. My body was, and is, the key to all of the moments, and yours is too. People like to talk about how our pets love us unconditionally. I get that. I have two dogs who think that I'm the sun, moon, and stars. But the body . . . your body and my body, and all of our bodies, they fight for us. They forgive every single mean act, neglectful act, abusive act, and painful act that we force them to endure. We no longer have to endure our bodies. We can honor and love our bodies and end the war. I'm not exactly sure how I came to a shift from self-loathing to self-respect, however, I knew that the war could end and that my kids and my life were waiting for me to quit swimming in shit. See, I was staying in the shit-filled pool hoping someone else would clean it up and do some maintenance. I wanted to be rescued and I wanted to have someone want to save me. What are we fighting for? It was my responsibility to first get out of the shitty pool and then to clean it up.

No one could do it for me.

Greatness is who you are. Greatness is your magnificent body. I know some people are born with a body that isn't textbook perfect, and so what. It's here. My body had cancer and I wouldn't want anyone else's. I really wouldn't. Some of you, as you read these words, might be thinking, *Yes but I don't have all of my limbs or I don't have all of my senses or I am in real physical pain or illness every damn day.* I am going to fight for your body as perfect, regardless. End the war. Start living in the body you have as much as you can. Or not, but at least consider the possibility that you could. Who are we honoring and what are we really proving living in a constant commitment to being anything other than our greatest self?

Your greatness is not you thinking you are better than anyone else, it's you committing right action for you and the life you want to live. The past is over. You made it. You won. You survived. Now *live.* Now, not later. Live your greatness. Be your greatness. We defend why we don't think we're great. We defend why we think we can't be great. This is okay if you want to be right about why you aren't great. Just know that the whole time you defend what isn't true about you, you are great regardless.

What's a vision? Vision comes from what you see as possible. Your vision is the future you see for yourself. What is the future that you see for yourself now? Does it match the future you want to be living? If yes, great, step into your greatness with support, and let's get a plan in place to help you get there! If not, then we need to address why it's more beneficial for you right now to be in a vision for the future you don't want. The good news here is that if you know the vision that you don't want, you can start to journal and dream about what the opposite would look and feel like. You are the expert on you that knows the future you want to live. I'm asking you to give up the fairy tale. Be brave enough to create your love story with your life. Your vision will either carry you into your pain or carry you out of your pain. You've got to focus on seeing yourself win, even if, especially if, you have zero evidence that you can. Of course you can.

Pain is a moment. It's time to get beyond what we think will feel better in a moment distracting us from the pain of how we've been living and to begin sculpting our lives like it's our greatest masterpiece. What helps is a vision. I needed a vision for my life beyond my childhood, beyond a marriage wracked with domestic violence, beyond leaving Las Vegas, and beyond cancer. You can have a new vision for your life because you decide that there is more life waiting for you.

Journal EXERCISE

- What would it be like to live into your greatness?

- What do you really want?

- What have you committed to in your past?

- What will you commit to next?

- How will making a commitment to the next thing you want change your life?

- Complete one act of greatness every day for ten days. Journal about your results and outcomes.

Chapter Eight

THE POSSIBILITIES

Decide to decide. Be willing to grow into your greatness. See beyond what you think will heal the pain. Regardless of what you saw or were told about what's possible for you, and no matter what you learned or experienced about life so far, it's time to change your mind if you want more life and more healing. Decisions, like life, are neutral. Life is not out to get you and cannot, like it or not, make you or break you. We blame and look for the scapegoat but it all comes down to will you decide or not? Your decisions got you here. What will you decide next? You are the ruler of your relationship with your experience of life and it's time to take the power back. Obviously, there is no one way or right way to decide. Slow way down with deciding so that you can go all in with each decision. This is how you win your way to happiness.

MIRRORS

Every wall is a mirror. I love visiting the ocean but I know this means I can't avoid the mirrors. Every single wall in the place is a mirror and all the windows give the most gorgeous view of the ocean. I hate mirrors. I love the ocean more than anything. My parents are living in Florida. I am clinically depressed and suicidal. The therapist talks about hospitalizing me but my charm and charisma, even through my depression, help me convince them that three days of therapy per week and antidepressants are a better solution. The hurricane-force intensity of my soul is stronger than the depression. But the mirrors have been my number one enemy. I live life "in spite of" what I see in the mirror. The therapy helps me start to see that I'm not crazy and that I have a lot of abuse to heal through. It also wakes me up to how fake I am being in my life. I'm like a chameleon trying to please and fit in. The thought of conflict is even worse than the mirrors. I believe that I can cause and make worse the inevitable conflicts that are brewing in my life and in my family. I want to be wrong about what I know was real about my childhood. I want to be wrong about my reality and that time in my life. I want to be right about my self-imposed job description that it's me who is supposed to keep the family together and make it all better.

Mirrors represent reality and I prefer la la land. I also run. Long runs along the ocean. Tears flow with each passing mile. I don't even know what I'm crying about most of the time. I can't stop. What I learn and what the therapists (I had two at once tag-teaming me, a man and a woman) help me discover is that feeling the emotions is the only way I will ever heal. It just doesn't make sense to me though because I don't think I need to heal anything. My life is *fine*! I am fine. I am at a good college, in the program I want to be in, doing well, with a good guy who I think loves me. I can fall into him as my safe place to fall. The Florida therapy this particular summer keeps me alive. I don't think I ever will ever actually attempt suicide, but I think about it constantly. I have a plan. I learn that if I don't face and feel, I will never heal. The mirrors represent my life, as it is, in all of its bittersweet reality.

Fast forward to the end of the summer which also means the end of the relationship with the Florida therapists. The note we end on is a disaster. I have avoided institutionalization and am feeling stronger and willing to go back to college while working with a new therapist. I am 135 pounds at this time which is my standard weight. The male Florida therapist sits me down as I transition out with my mother and me, and tells me that if I would lose weight, I would feel better. My mom and the women in my family are so thin and I'm not. He says casually, "If you got thin too you would be happier." He tells me that I should fast and only eat vegetables if I have to eat anything at all until I get to a "reasonable weight." My mother nods and agrees with the therapist—his solution to my pain is that I should lose weight. She tries to talk me into it after we leave the office driving down A1A. Beachfront Avenue is full of hard bodies and glamor and luckily, I have the wherewithal to know that the therapist's advice is total horseshit. I will never see that therapist again. My years of bulimia and my love affair with purging begin the fall after this summer. I am also over-exercising and taking pills to help me lose weight faster and I begin to restrict what I eat. On some level I take the advice of the therapist without even realizing it. I have never gone into a full-blown eating disorder before this time in my life. I have a history of body image issues, for sure. I have negative, even toxic self-talk with my body. But things were about to escalate.

⤬

All this was me eating my pain. How much of your life have you spent eating your pain instead of facing it, feeling it and talking about it? What if telling your truth about what's going on in and with you, could never ever hurt anyone? Your truth about others is a different story. Stick to your truth about you and know that even if that triggers someone else, they are feeling something that was buried in them long before anything you said or did and it's just projection. Risk telling your truth or at the very least acknowledging it within yourself. That just can't and won't hurt anything or anyone and it will help you see so much clearer. It's refusing to feel and refusing to talk that is hurting you on a soul level and from there your life takes hit after hit. It got to the point where in a kickboxing class one day that year in college, I passed out. I couldn't understand why. Then it got worse. In the middle of sex one day, I passed out, fell off the bed, and had a seizure. My boyfriend rushed me to the hospital and they ran all kinds of tests. I was malnourished, given fluids, and then got sent home. I still didn't "wake up." I wouldn't wake up and snap back to reality. I was addicted to my favorite meal called hate myself. What I was feeding myself was a diet of "It's all your fault," "You're too fat," "You don't get to be happy," "You are the cause of pain," "You are too much," "Stop being too much." "Something is wrong with you." I still wouldn't wake up to the reality of what I was doing to my poor body that was fighting so hard for me. It took more than *fifteen years* for me and stage 3 cancer for me to really come out of this. What's your poison? What limited possibilities have you been living in that are holding you back?

LOOK BEHIND THE WALLS

Every wall is a mirror. This is such a great metaphor. Every perceived wall has more possibility behind it. Walls show up where we are blocked, where we are afraid, and where we haven't created new evidence that we can go further than we think we can. Conflict isn't meant to be avoided and owning our impact is everything. What I mean by that is we can be the force that knocks our pain or new possibility into motion. How do you get over the walls? Start by embracing conflict and triggers knowing that there is possibility on the other side.

Let's start with triggers. They are access points that provide an opening to healing and breakthrough when we're brave enough to explore them. Try saying to yourself, "I've got this energy, this belief, this story, and this old wound that no longer serves me. This trigger is bubbling up because it's time for me to heal and release the stuck emotion underneath it." This process will give you power back instead of triggers having power over you. What would your life be like if you learned how to have power over your triggers in any and all scenarios? No matter what darkness or triggers show up, there's always a beginning, a middle, and an end to the emotional discomfort that we don't want to feel. When we lean in, breathe into the pain, and stay with it until the emotional charge starts to relax, we get power back. With commitment, and courage to feel, eventually, triggers can be released.

Understand that prioritizing avoiding conflict only creates more conflict. Life has seasons. Some can be more challenging than others for some people. The season of winter, especially. Winter is a season that wipes the slate clean. The trees let go. The flowers hibernate. And the sun still comes out day after day as preparation for rebirth begins. Heading into the holidays, into winter, and heading into the darker parts of the year, I invite you to get willing to face conflict in a new way. Allow yourself to prepare for rebirth, too. To sit with what you want to grow in you and for your life next. Allow yourself to let go of what's not a part of that next piece of your vision. And know that it's okay and actually critical to include letting go of the triggers that don't fit the picture for where your life is headed as well. This next season, choose to be someone who will be who it takes to deal with and be with conflict and triggers as they arise. You can deal with, face, or move through and conquer the conflict in your life. I know you can. Conflict isn't bad or wrong. Conflict can create more connection when we use it as an opportunity to learn and understand ourselves and other people. Conflict means it's time for a growth spurt, every time. See conflict in a new light. Because the conflicts will continue to pop up like Whac-A-Mole as you continue to step into more and more life. That's not because of anything you've done, it's because the version of you that was living one way is now ready to live in another way. That's the conflict to focus on. You with you.

If we lean in, breathe into it and stay with triggers and conflict until the charge starts to relax, it eventually releases and goes away. I want people to understand that the goal is not to try to avoid conflict. That's what so many people do and it limits possibility more than anything else. I want you to learn how to make your triggers your bitch instead of them having a hold over you. I want you to learn how to embrace possibility in the face of uncomfortable emotions and uncomfortable scenarios so that no matter what you're facing, you never lose sight of the fact that there is more waiting for you on the other side of the wall. No more trying to do damage control or tolerating until it gets so painful that it seems like you are now forced to show up and deal with it. We all have our vices that keep us from possibility. Those vices and the triggers and conflicts that occur can show you so much if you will look at them, bravely, in the mirror. Once you see it you get power back, so fast. And you can say to your-self, *All right, I've got this energy, this belief, this story, this old wound that no longer serves me that is literally bubbling up because it's time for me to release it.*

Our triggers really and truly do run our lives if we're not aware and if we're not careful. Your triggers, the things in you, the things in others that get you feeling shaken, those triggers become patterns that run your life in different costumes, in different flavors, with different characters until you take on being willing to be with them, leaning in, breathing in, sitting in it, as long as it takes again for that energy to start to relax. And if you can trust and know that there's life on the other side of the trigger, not meaning, *Oh, the trigger went away and it's dealt with for now,* but there's literally life on the other side of the trigger, meaning you've broken through the pattern so that it's no longer a thing. It is possible for you to make your triggers less and less painful and to integrate healing your triggers so they never seem more powerful than you are. It's possible for you to learn how to relax into them so that you can use them to experience more life instead of less.

I want you to consider that life isn't happening to you. It's also not happening *for* you. Life is neutral. Life just happens and none of it is more powerful or more capable than you are. As I've said, life will go your way and it won't go your way and none of that is about you, it's just life. It's an interesting dance with conflict, isn't it? We can't avoid it. We also can't survive without it if we want to grow and get the most out of life. Every time it's time for another growth spurt, we can look in the mirror and get through another level of conflict. What I'm offering is a new way of seeing conflict. You get to choose the relationship that we have with it.

HOW WE NAVIGATE CONFLICT IS BREAKTHROUGH WORK

In simple terms, breakthrough means that you've moved beyond triggers and your fear of getting through conflict. I see triggers as avoidance of our truth. If we are being the source of our own encouragement, committed to our next dream and vision of where we want our lives to go, knowing why it's important to us, we cannot be threatened. Yes, I'm suggesting that you can get so clear and committed (which is what breakthrough is) that you can't be threatened at your essence by anything outside of you. Breakthrough just means unlimited. Nothing is in the way of commitment when we're in breakthrough. When you fall into old patterns of fight, flight, freeze, otherwise known as survival mode, you know a breakthrough into more possibility is needed. And a breakthrough to possibility is always available. When life hits us with new triggers, or old triggers, fear takes over, and our brains go into wanting to fight, run, or wanting to shut down, it's important to know that emotional breakthrough is another option. We get to have a breakthrough life but not if we shut down, even just a little.

The most dangerous thing anybody can do emotionally, by the way, is shut down and freeze. That is the beginning of a slow spiritual death that could lead to actual death. And then there's flight, where we just run away. We get busy. We numb out; we brush it under the carpet. We'll do anything but face the emotional pain. That's always the problem. What's always the issue is the emotional experience that you're having, never the circumstance. Finally, fight is just resistance that has us out of control and stuck. No matter how hard we fight, we can't change our circumstances. The more resistance we have, the more we swim upstream instead of breaking through to make room for ease and flow.

Breathe into the possibility of break through. It's a beginning. I've created a road map for me to break through into more and more life whenever I want more freedom, and you can create one for yourself too. I've vehemently committed to a breakthrough life. This keeps me moving forward and keeps me at least paying attention to accessing the highest version of me that is there every step of the way. I believe with all my heart that I am healthy and deserving of the most beautiful life and my greatest wish is that you will make this decision for yourself too. At the very least I ask you to be in this question as much as possible until life feels the way you want it to, "How am I living?"

When we're living in such a way where we need the entire world to be how we need it to be for us to be okay, we're totally screwed because life's going to happen. I say this a lot: life is going to go your way . . . *and* it's not. None of this is about you. It's just life. Breakthrough means you've connected to an opening, even if it's small or feels insignificant. In breakthrough we have control over how we navigate, outwit, outsmart, outlast, and conquer fear. That is the game: the emotional work. Because it's never other people or the situation that is the cause of your fear, upsets, and triggers. You've got everything you need to break through. I'm certain of it. It's like an eighth gear that we all have that we don't know we have. I'm here today to tell you there's life beyond fight-flight-freeze, there's life beyond survival. It's called *breakthrough*.

Your relationship with triggers and conflict is no one's fault. Your relationship with breakthrough is 100 percent your responsibility. Regardless of what you saw or were told about conflict, and no matter what you learned or experienced about conflict, you made up your mind about what conflict is and what it means to you. Life is neutral. It's not out to get you and cannot, like it or not, make you or break you. Now that we've established that you are the ruler of your relationship with conflict, it's time to take the power back. I'll let you in on what's worked for me. What's worked for me is to slow way down with when I notice a trigger or conflict. I'm taking in the experience in my body. I'm paying attention to my emotions. I am paying attention to how I feel, what I want, what I need, and what is scaring me. If we weren't scared there would be no conflict because we would be navigating the situation free of fear and triggers.

Slow down. Slow down not just when you are upset but as a practice. That is how you can start to see the red flags leading up to the triggers that lead to the conflict that you haven't broken through yet. Moving through conflict into breakthrough can be a sacred ritual. I have friends who thank the farmers honoring where the food came from before every meal. I love that and try to remember as much as I can to follow suit with food and with conflict. I honor where it came from. I learned it. My coping skills kept me alive. But now I want more than survival. I want a new sacred and spiritual awakening with every wall and every conflict that appears. As counterintuitive as it might seem, I'm asking you to respectfully take in conflict and triggers and from there do the work to break through. Plenty of people have made millions trying to sell the world on managing patterns and pain with mindset and strategy work. It's not enough. Breakthrough is the secret-sauce formula for coming back to life. I want you to have this tool in your back pocket.

You are worthy. You've done your best. You've tried it all, nutrition, therapy, books, school, trying harder, trying everything. Breakthrough is a new way to live. A breakthrough life is waiting for you. A life where you live how you want to live. A life that fits in with you. You do belong here, in this life. You do fit into the world as the unique and gorgeous soul that you are. And it's time to turn the page. Are you willing to turn the page and begin to actually let yourself have, experience and enjoy happiness? There's nothing to prove just life to enjoy, love, and live. It's about damn time that you feel comfortable in your own skin, in your one precious life. You are so valuable. Not because of what you do but because of who you are. You know what you want. Deep down maybe but it's in there. You do know what matters and is most important to you, really. On some level you must know that you are not here to be normal, you are here to experience and know what you are capable of and how powerful, loved and deserving you are.

THE ROPES COURSE

My hands feel and grip the metal. Wind is whipping and I keep looking at the giant rock on my finger. It isn't mine but I have it on my person, for now. I am on my hands and knees gripping the wire holding me 50 feet up off the ground. I had almost fallen. Almost. But I caught myself. Somehow I know how strong I am. I know I can catch myself and not fall. I have to make it across. For some reason, climbing up the 50-foot high telephone pole was the easy part. One foot, one hand, the other foot, the other hand. I have a focus line. It's a cord that is my lifeline on this event, in this seminar. The focus line is unsteady because my focus is unsteady.

I am in Utah in the middle of nowhere on a ropes course setting goals and wanting so much more. This is the biggest goal yet. I want to be a happily married woman. My coach and facilitator of this high ropes course seminar has us declaring what we want before we have it. We're instructed to say what we want as if it's already happened and manifested, no matter how impossible it seems. I desperately want to be married again and happy. It has to exist, right? The wind is so intense. I say under my breath, "I am a happily married woman. I am a happily married woman." The wire isn't tougher than I am. I hold on. I cling tightly. Then I slip. I fall. But I grab on as the tears come hard and fast. Through the tears, slowly, I crawl my way, bloody and bruised, across the wire and make it to the other pole. "I am a happily married woman."

The reason I share this story is because at the time I was so sure that this dream was impossible. How could you be happy and married? I had never seen it and my first shot at marriage ended in disaster with so much collateral damage. But I wanted it. I desperately wanted to be a happily married woman. I wanted it so much. I wanted a family. I wanted to be happy. I wanted to be free. I wanted to be joyful. But it was so far from my picture of possibility. And the sex had to be better than great too. Why settle for less? As a single mom of a little girl who I wanted to give the entire world to, I wanted her to grow up in a happy family. I made it 50 feet up the telephone pole and across the 50-foot high wire that represented the journey that I would have to take to get from where I was to where I wanted to be. I recognized, higher up than I was comfortable with, that this is life. My only option was to start where I was and from there, I would have to be the one to get through, even if that meant crawling on hands and knees, bleeding and bruised, to my goal.

Today I have been blessed to know that a happy marriage is more than possible. I learned how to navigate partnership with new rules with my second husband. The number one rule is to be self-responsible for breaking through triggers and upsets so that we can experience new possibilities separately and together. We embrace conflict, and have a rule that conflict brings us closer together. And it does! We've been through so much together, both weighed down by stress, life, and cancer, while pregnant.

AWARENESS IS EVERYTHING

How many moments have you missed, just going through the motions waiting for the next season instead of loving and living in the season that you're in now? How much pressure have you put on yourself and on other people to help you feel better? Now that you are aware, please be gentle with yourself. You didn't mean to put pressure on others or life. Forgive yourself for doing the best you could with the tools that you had. Now you have new tools. The thing is, it's not too much work to become more aware. It's actually such an incredible amount of work to ignore taking on your relationships with triggers, conflict, and upsets. Everything you experience really does matter because from a woke place of being fully awake and aware to *what is happening inside of you*, you get to craft the experiences that you want to be having. *It's not your fault but it is your work.* Breakthrough is medicine and it's the solution to self-medicating, self-abandonment, self-betrayal, and self-harm. Breakthrough means ultimate freedom and the best kind of self-loving badassery.

Journal EXERCISE

- Make a poster representing you as the source of your own encouragement and put it up somewhere in your home. Look at it daily as a gentle reminder that the life you want is your responsibility to create.

- Track your triggers. In a journal, note when you are triggered. What is happening? What are you feeling? What patterns do you notice? Bring this journal to therapy or coaching to dive deeper into your healing.

Chapter Nine

THE FORGIVENESS

Pour into me love.

Pour into me your truth.

Pour into me your most vivid and intoxicatingly enticing fantasies.

Pour into me your heart and your laughter.

Pour into me your heartbreak and the bitter taste of your tears.

Pour into me every word you have not been able to speak.

Pour into me every wish that's on the tip of your tongue.

I hear you.

I can taste it.

I will honor you.

I will show you the way.

You are the love of my life.

Love,

Your Life

IT'S NOT YOUR FAULT

Sitting at another red light, I'm impatient and frustrated. I don't have time for this. Feeling a little sick, congested, tired, and fatigued, *I don't have time for this.* I am already feeling behind schedule. I wonder when I will finally get "there" to the place where I feel enough, like what I have created and lived for is enough. There is so much to do. There isn't enough time. This is how pre-cancer Rebeccah used to think pretty much daily. For many years I didn't get sick. I'm not sure why. I was pushing my body to the limit. Drinking too much. Getting only three to four hours of sleep at night. Working three jobs and trying to win at super single mom life. Those years I prided myself on how much I was running (50 to 60 miles a week) while I was running on fumes. I would tell people I don't get sick, almost bragging. And I didn't. Until I did. My naturalist oncologist told me in my first meeting with her that the body gets sick in an effort to buffer, like Netflix, to go from feeling sluggish and behind to getting back into ahead-of-the-game mode. She suggested to me, which went against everything that I had ever believed or thought prior, that I knew about wellness, that when the body was sick it was **working.** This was shocking to me. But it also made a lot of sense and helped me make peace pretty quickly with the fact that I had a cancer diagnosis. It helped me to begin the process of surrendering into forgiveness: forgiveness of self-destructive and survival-mode choices. Forgiveness for all of the times that I wished, even begged, to die. What would life be like if it was okay to embrace the idea that my body was working for me and working perfectly when I got sick? I didn't get sick until I blew out my adrenals completely and worked myself into a state of go-go-go to the point where inevitably I had to crash. Cancer was a reboot. It wasn't my fault but it was a wake-up call. And as the human being that I am, of course I'm going to get sick. We get sick so that we can recalibrate. Now when I hear people brag about not getting sick, I don't get jealous. I am concerned for them. When I wasn't getting sick, I was pretty much in a state of shock and a permanent adrenaline rush. This wasn't healthy or worth bragging about since the joke was on me. I say that in jest; the cancer was no joke but I was in a huge lie that I could abuse my body and not have it get to a breaking point. Another lie was that I deserved to be so mean to and hard on myself.

Do you pay attention to and notice what's going on around you with the way people treat themselves and each other? Have you ever thought about, really, what you are putting yourself through and how hard you are on yourself? Do you know what it's costing you? How do you feel watching those you love, or even strangers for that matter, as they crucify themselves or give up on themselves? How many conversations do you have on a daily basis where you or someone else is commenting on their faults and defending their stress levels?

Once upon a time it didn't even occur to you to talk shit to yourself or to anyone else. When did it get so easy and normal to slam ourselves and each other? What I'm about to say is not rocket science but it is real, for me anyway. When we're suffering, we're defending life the way we don't want it to be. We defend the relationship with ourselves that we don't want every time we say anything even close to negative about ourselves or another. You as the main character of your life is the closest thing to a real best friend that you'll ever have. What else? Who else is there for you 100 percent of the time? Every time you tell yourself you don't have time to take care of you, or when you tell yourself and believe the lie that you can't afford to take care of getting your needs met, you rob yourself of your most beautiful future and of being fully alive.

Forgiveness is a process. It's so much easier to see what we don't want or all the reasons why we think that something won't work out. I want you to give yourself permission now to start seeing yourself, really seeing yourself, *in the life that you ultimately want.* From there, you can start to see yourself really living the life you want. My experience has been that if I see it, from where I am now, how I want it now, whatever "it" is, transformation happens faster. Caution: once it becomes clear that you could have what you want or that things can be different for you, within you, now, that's when we can start to really go off on ourselves. How did I not see this? I could have had this all along? Forgiveness is about letting your best at the time be enough. It's about lovingly and with great compassion embracing your humanity while you step into free will and agency as you choose new and right for you moving forward. But let's really dive into forgiveness so that we can feel even better about who we've been and where we are now as we design our next season.

Forgiveness gives you closure and inner peace without needing things or people to have been different. *Understand that no one ever has the power to emotionally hurt you. They are showing you your unhealed emotional wounds that can and deserve to heal.* People aren't wrong or bad, and they are doing the best they can at their level of awareness, too. They are also playing out what has happened and may still be unhealed from their past when they are behaving in a way that is cruel. I want us all to have standards on how we want to be treated and boundaries that support those standards. Your standards deserve to be met and will be met by those ready to support you.

But how do we forgive, especially the seemingly unforgivable? Instead of focusing on what happened or whether or not the person or people involved deserve to be forgiven, focus on your right to experience inner peace and self-love no matter what the situation is. Consider that abuse, trauma, disease, death, and tragedy do not have to define you or ruin the rest of your life. You deserve to be free and can be free if you will forgive in two ways. First, you must forgive yourself for doing the best you could in the circumstances. Maybe you didn't speak up or take action, or maybe you became aggressive, or maybe you ghosted. Whatever it is, you did your best. Learn from your mistakes. Love yourself anyway. From there, see the people involved as human and doing their best, too. Forgive them for their humanity, set your boundaries, and allow them to grow with you or not. The point is they can't make you feel less than. Forgive them so that you get back to the best of you, for you. Let people love you, their way, and keep your standards high.

Here are a few hacks:

FORGIVENESS HACK #1. When you are hurt, do the inner work to heal through the emotional pain that is stuck underneath the hurt.

FORGIVENESS HACK #2. Love as much and as hard as you did before you got hurt—for you, not them.

FORGIVENESS HACK #3. See people as innocent, starting with yourself.

Forgiveness is a way to get back to peace within yourself. Inner peace, regardless of circumstances, trauma, and how you have been treated, is possible if you will be brave enough to forgive yourself for your part in the scenario while forgiving the people involved for being who they were, and how they were, at their level of awareness. You don't need the other person involved to practice forgiveness. Forgiveness is an internal practice of getting back to a place and space of love in you.

Forgiveness is the gateway to self-love, closure, and inner peace. Forgiveness means to get back to loving freely without walls, guardedness, or fear running the show. It's simple, not easy, and always worth it. Forgiveness is for you and benefits everyone when you get emotionally free and clear because from there you get back to being the best of yourself. Forgiveness means loving yourself first, without shame, flaws and all, as much or more than you did before whatever happened. From there, love the other person, human to human, as much as you did before the hurt, meaning you kept your heart open. And set boundaries, maintain standards, and take no crap. You can be the best of you, for you, so you can have the experience of closure and inner peace that you deserve.

FORGIVENESS IS SEXY

Have you considered that where you hurt, there is emotional hurt there? It will not kill you to allow your emotions to move through you. The thing is your emotions can't hurt anyone. "Feeling" isn't violent and if you are feeling your emotions in a healthy way, you are getting them out. Let it out, all the way out, without lashing out or directing your pain at another person so that you can forgive yourself. Forgiveness means full trust. When you forgive yourself, you trust that it's safe for you to love fully and to be loved fully. Be the one who is brave enough to break the cycle. That's super sexy. Just please don't be shame-based about your healing and forgiveness work. We have a picture in our mind of how we think our lives should look and feel. Stop fighting feeling your way through the pain that would get you there.

The love that your life has for you is immeasurable. Once you surrender into that, your life and your pain will transform. The world keeps turning while billions sit around hating themselves. There was a time when you trusted yourself. We don't need to trust other people. They are human and doing the best that they can, too. We need to trust ourselves by trusting our intentions and by knowing on a soul level that we are doing the best we can. My dream is that as a collective humanity we will learn how to heal through our triggers, taking responsibility for emotional healing, and doing forgiveness work to break through survival so that we can be clear as the best of ourselves, compassionately caring about each other as much as ourselves from that clear place.

There was a time when your life didn't hurt. You were not born heartbroken or in emotional pain. Let's go into it. Where does it hurt? When did it start hurting? When did you decide that you needed protection and from what? I know you got hurt. Me too. I get it but let's live anyway. Be sexy anyway. Your body is carrying the fear of getting hurt again and if you don't relax and let go of self-protection, you are just training the universe to keep making sure that you need more and more evidence that life is something to protect yourself from. We don't have to hurt. It's unnecessary. Life doesn't have to be painful. Love doesn't have to be painful. If we won't feel all of it, the dark *and* the light, we suffer. Pay attention to where you are still hurting. And then forgive yourself.

Here is a process for you:
Begin by breathing into the pain.

Now listen to your body: notice where in your body you feel stuck or blocked.

Find the pain in your body.

Tell the pain, "Thank you for trying to protect me."

Tell the pain, "I don't need you anymore, you can go back now to where you came from."

Now let yourself cry, scream, laugh, or simply just breathe the pain out of your body (tension in the body comes from holding our breath).

Let it go.

Say out loud five times, "I forgive myself for holding onto the pain and for living in survival mode."

Allow yourself to be proud of yourself—you've made it this far.

Celebrate and invite yourself to begin to enjoy your life.

Let yourself get excited about life again.

Say out loud five times, "I forgive myself because I love myself."

GET INTENTIONAL

The most important gift you can give yourself is to get very intentional. The opposite of being intentional is blowing in the wind, going through the motions. When it comes to your life, please don't just blow in the wind. Try paying more attention to whether or not you are being intentional moment to moment. Turn up your awareness. Get out of "autopilot" mode so that you can finally win at your ability to have control over the parts of your life you have control over. Life happens, we know that. There is so much we have no control over no matter how hard we try. But we always have control over whether or not we're being intentional about whether or not we are in a commitment to breakthrough, whether we've forgiven ourselves, and whether or not we're being intentional about where our lives are going next. The most important choice that you can make and the most important gift you can give yourself in any given moment is to be intentional. How can you get more intentional when making a choice? Pay attention. Ask yourself, *Is this choice going to bring me more freedom?* This is one simple tool that you can add to your toolkit right now.

Intentional choice can change the course of your entire life. I want freedom for you, and too many of you are not feeling free. Too many of you are feeling stressed, suffocated, and maybe even stuck. Freedom is so close. It's right here. Forgiving yourself and getting intentional is a personal practice and process. No one can tell you how to do it. And no one can tell you what your specific needs or wants are, or what the next right choice and intention for you is. Just be more aware and practice. Slow down first. Then listen. Then absorb what you heard your inner guidance system whispering to you. Give yourself the gift of getting intentional about how you are living.

WHAT YOU CAN CONTROL

What would your life be like if you just decided to give up control over all of that outside noise and got intentional instead? This means to let go of what's not yours to carry, yours to stress over (and nothing is worth stressing over), or yours to try to fix (because nothing is broken). The world will keep spinning. When I came out of cancer, a whole year had flown by. I remember thinking, *Wow, I lost a whole year.* I call it my cancer coma year. There was so much fog and so much life had happened around me while I was fighting for my life. The show really does go on when we let life do its thing. How heavy does it feel to try to white knuckle and force your way into other people's lives and into life's natural process and flow?

This doesn't mean just stop showing up for others, not at all. I am suggesting that we can all be more present with what is truly our responsibility to control. For example, you control your food, your sleep, hydration, sex, how much time you give and to what, whether or not you are taking care of your house, your car, your things, how you are being in your relationships, whether or not you listen, whether or not you lead or avoid, whether or not you are committed to your pain or your freedom. See how this works? At the end of the day, you control how you showed up. Period. The rest happens or happened or is happening. Then you get to choose how you will show up to the party of your life. Get out of everyone else's life and their choices and get committed to your own. We focus on others because it's an easy distraction. It's a no-win situation, though.

You get to live your life, have your life, and enjoy indulgences. The problem is that we seek solace and comfort instead of getting intentional and speaking up, or making choices that actually honor us and how we want to live. How we want to live in our own lives is often contradicted by our need for small comforts to avoid feeling our heartbreak or disappointment. When heartbreak strikes, that's the time to step into, not out of, what you have control over—which is getting more intentional, not less.

YOU MAKE THE RULES

I made a rule with myself years ago that I would never drink alcohol to drown my sorrows. I knew that would just be a way to numb out and distract myself from what I want to feel, and then my body would have to absorb my emotional pain, and the alcohol, and the words I wouldn't say. Can you say heavy? I drink to celebrate, in moderation, or I don't drink. I'm not saying this should be a rule for you but it's an *intentional* rule I have with me. Here are some more examples. I made another rule with myself years ago to not take my emotions out on others. I have another rule with myself that I take responsibility for my emotions and my experience. I look at my part in my relationships and results. I want to be my best and choose to live as my best.

As adults we truly do get to make our own rules. I know it often doesn't feel like it, but we really do get to choose in absolutely every single moment of our lives. I look at the rules I have with myself as the scaffolding I need to set up the strongest foundation possible for my life. Other people do not need to follow or agree with my rules, for me, but I need to be consistent and follow through on what I know works for me so that I can trust myself. Make sense? We all tick differently. Different rules, and soul food, for different folks. But do you know yours? Do you have any? In your choices notice whether or not you are you moving toward, or away from, the life that you are so very much wanting, seeking, and striving toward. I have a rule that I am clean and clear with me. What that means to me is no regrets, no withholds, no toxic icky energy with me. I face triggers and do the work to break through. I'm willing to do whatever it takes to grow with people as long as they are willing to work on the relationship with me.

Do you want to be the dragon food or do you want to slay the dragon? What's your dragon? We get so used to our dragons that we don't even realize that they are illusions. You can beat them. One of my dragons was being afraid to believe post cancer that my body would get strong again. The doctors told me I'd never walk again normally. I went into pre-menopause, adrenal failure, and my hormones were barely functional, let alone optimally running, to support weight loss. There were years where I just gave up hoping I could "get out of physical pain." I rationalized that I was lucky to be alive. The truth was I was just scared. Scared to try and fail. Scared to believe that I could ever feel healthy again. This has been one of the biggest dragons of my life. Today my hormones are strong. My body is strong. I walk, hike, strength train, do yoga and ride my Peloton religiously. It's an ongoing commitment and intention to be healthy, feel healthy, and to keep getting stronger.

WHY YOU AREN'T HAPPY

Actions and doing more isn't it. Get intentional now, not just about what you are creating in terms of results, but also what you are creating in terms of how you are experiencing your life. Of course action and effort is required when we are committed to growth. It's more than action though, so much more. Change and growth start with intention that takes you in the right direction. If you can't see it, you certainly won't be creating it anytime soon. If we won't love and embrace where we are, the fight continues. It's a fight with ourselves with life as it is now.

As you maintain momentum and a constant focus on your future that includes the life you want, you can't lose, as long as you stay in the game. We don't need a different life. Use the life you have. You've earned the life you want, intention will help you get there. Intention is what you can control and it's what it takes to get all that you are desiring. There is nothing wrong with desire. There is nothing wrong with allowing yourself to outgrow the life you are currently living. It's not that we outgrow our life or people or the season we are in; we evolve. Evolution requires transformation and it won't happen overnight. It also won't happen if you fight your desires. We are either committed to growth or we are defending where we are. Defending where we are hurting is not a fun life. Many choose to live wishing and hoping or in a hamster wheel. The way to grow is to get out of to-do list mode and to relax into your truth. From there it's about being who you need to be to get to where you know you are headed, because you've decided that you won't *not* get there. If you don't know where you are headed, you'll stay in the hamster wheel. You will stay spinning. You will lose at your dreams.

It's time to stop forcing and manipulating our way around what it is we see for ourselves in this one life. Go for it. There will be tears. There will be laughter too. There will be wins along the way. Just be careful not to avoid your emotions. You can enjoy life as it is now as you intentionally live into your next level, creating life as you want it to be.

SAY YOU'RE SORRY

Have you apologized to yourself yet? Like really apologized? Have you looked into your eyes and connected with the pain your body is holding? Have you acknowledged all of the moments where you were mean? How many times have you ignored your own needs and signals? How many times have you refused to listen to your soul's screams? But what about the moments where it does feel like too much? If those moments come, they will also go by. When it feels like it's all too much, focus on what it is that you do not want to face or feel. Sit with it. Breathe into it. Then forgive yourself for your part in the situation. Then start to visualize life on the other side of the wall in front of you. From there get intentional and commit to getting to the other side as long as it takes, whatever it takes.

Your confidence will come back. Here's a fun exercise. How do you want your life talked about? Write it out. What do you want people to say about you when you are not in the room? Next get intentional about who you will have to be for those conversations to happen. Here's a hint, start talking to yourself and about yourself the way that you just wrote about. We think we can't risk living in hell and losing it all while we've already lost it all by giving ourselves up and selling out on the life we really want. Then we take it out on others.

For now, even though it may sound odd, be loving to your negative thoughts. The more we resist what is, the bigger and louder it gets. Remind yourself: *I have been using shut down and busy as coping skills (or whatever it is for you) and now I'm going to find a better way to get my needs met.* It takes great courage to make a different choice. What if you dropped "making yourself wrong" for good? Your experience is real. Your feelings are real. Fear, anger, grief, excitement and joy are real and healthy, and not drama. You can be happy even if people around you are not. You can forgive yourself even if other people won't. Figure out what you need in those moments of upset that you are not getting. Avoidance won't work. What are you avoiding? Love yourself! You are so, so, worth it.

We don't need a drama or to blow our lives up so that we can decide now is the time to take our power back, or to take the lead, or to have what we want. So many of us wait until a crisis point to choose to move in a new direction. Some people even blow up their entire lives to give themselves permission to move in a new direction, especially during the pandemic. It doesn't have to be this way. As my husband says, "You get to choose your rock bottom." In other words, you get to choose the moment, the now, when you are going to take your life back.

GET CONFIDENT

Confidence happens when you are committed to closing the gap between where you are and where you want to be. It's scary to be confident when you are in new and unfamiliar territory but confidence is the exact ingredient needed to get over every wall in front of you. Confidence means clarity. Getting clear and intentional about what you want and then knowing you are going to make it happen builds confidence. My big ask is that you choose to be confident that you can lead and handle anything that comes your way, because you can. That's a great place to start. When you aren't confident you are looking for evidence that things are not going to work out. It's also a symptom of not believing you can make it happen. Whether or not you are committed to moving through the very real conflicts and obstacles that stand between you and your goal is the determining factor of whether or not you will become confident.

Arrogance comes from fear. Confidence comes from clarity and commitment before you know it's going to happen or work out. Be confident about your ability to learn, grow, and adapt. You have evidence to support this already. You've survived 100 percent of what you've been through. We know what to do to maintain the lives we have. We don't know we have what it takes—yet—to get to the next level. We have to become the source of our own confidence. Needing validation from others and the world will keep your confidence shaky, at best. You build confidence by being committed to doing whatever it takes, as long as it takes, even with the voices in your head, the haters and critics, laughing at you. You keep going anyway, despite no evidence that you are going to make it.

Here are a few confidence hacks:

CONFIDENCE HACK #1. Use the word *yet* when you doubt yourself. I don't have enough courage, yet. I don't have the new job, yet. I don't have enough money, yet. I don't have a great relationship, yet. My body isn't where I want it to be, yet.

CONFIDENCE HACK #2. Decide that you do have what it takes. You have what it takes to create a life you love, I promise. All it takes is a decision to do whatever it takes, as long as it takes, to get through whatever life throws your way until you cross the finish line.

Choose one thing you are confident about, and when all else fails remember that. For example, I am confident that I don't need life to be different in the hard moments. It's hard because it's new and I don't have evidence, yet, that I have what it takes. I am confident in my capacity to learn, heal, and grow through anything and everything that shows up in my life. Or, I am confident that I did my best. Or, I am confident that there is a lesson here for me to learn. Confidence comes from being intentional, knowing what you want, knowing why you want it, and committing to making it happen. When you know who you are, what is important to you, and trust yourself to do what you say you will do, confidence grows.

Play your life like you have nothing to lose. The only thing you have to lose is you. Don't you dare let that happen. Let love in. Let people love you their way today, not the way you think they should. This includes letting life love you and loving it back. Time isn't a constraint, and life isn't a constraint. What time is, is your privilege. Lead intentionally and confidently every moment of your life as much as you can. Get through the moment focused on where you are heading. Your truth will change in the next moment, that's perfectly natural. Like nature has different weather moment to moment, we are different from moment to moment. And remember that there is never a moment where you are not emotional, this is good news. You are alive. *Live.*

There is no need to present a false image of who you are ever again. We don't lose our voices, we stop talking. It's insane, simply the craziest kind of cuckoo bird bat shit crazy, to live and not be who you are. I want to know who you are. It's never been that the world can't handle you. It's that you couldn't handle being you. I'm going to suggest that this is the worst kind of self-inflicted hell to live in. Every moment and every opportunity are yours for the taking but we wait. For what? For a sign? For permission? For the sky to fall or for the apocalypse? This is your life. What will you do with it? Find your audience. Find your people. Create a cocoon of support. Have the *right* support. Say your truth that no one else can say. Tell the world what you want to say, then at least you will know that you did. Your only job is to live fully, now, not later.

This is your moment. This is your time. Please risk the world's reaction. You can't know what will happen but at least there will never be the question of, What if? What if I said what I really felt? What if I risked being who I am in this lifetime while I am healthy, alive, and able? What if I was willing to set the bar as high as possible in this lifetime? In this moment. In this year. In this marriage. In this job. While my kids are still small. You've got it in you to thrive. The only question is, will you? If you were going to thrive in this life, how would that feel? What would you do? Who would you be? How would you LIVE? All I ask is that you get awake enough and intentional enough that you know that you get to choose. You get to choose, just like you get to live. There is always an answer and it will always be you. Your heart matters. Your voice matters. Your life matters. Now what? No what ifs. No do overs. Just this moment and the next choice. All you need is you, clear intention, a vision, confidence, and someone to do your work in front of. You don't need to know how. You don't need to know why. You don't need to know when. Decide who you will be now and in the next moment and then in the next moment. Fly. Fly higher. Fly even higher, your way.

THE ASSAULT

It felt like I must have had a tattoo on my forehead that said, "You can fuck with me. Literally." It had been several months of living successfully as a single mom and I was doing it. I made ends meet working three jobs and we were getting by. I was starting to relax into my new reality and I decided to run a marathon as my divorce therapy. Somehow I made time for every training run and I felt stronger. I felt like I could breathe when I ran. I decided that instead of running away from my pain and my past, it was time to run toward my future. I was ready for the race and friends came with me on the road trip of our lives. Another car ride that would never be forgotten and this one would stay with all of us for our lifetimes. Long story short, we never made it to that race because of a snowstorm. The hotel we stayed in was the only one in town and we were basically trapped, roads closed going both ways for forty-eight hours. There would be no race therapy for me that weekend. I was so disappointed! I will never forget the heaviness of that disappointment. At least the hotel had a treadmill. So, I decided to run. I did a fourteen-mile maintenance run that day and signed up for a different marathon in the town I was living in four weeks later. There are pictures of me running on the treadmill that day, sweaty and surrendering. I couldn't change the situation but I could run and I could find another race. My friends were supportive and loving and we did our best to get through that weekend. I didn't realize I was being watched in a way that would change my life forever. There were windows and the treadmill was close to the main lobby so I saw hotel staff, walk by every so often, but I thought nothing of it.

It was a small town and a small hotel. We made the best of it. An employee of the hotel took special interest in me. By the end of the second night, he was talking about taking me to Paris and falling in love. I started to feel dizzy and sick and wanted the night to end. I desperately wanted to forget about this terrible weekend, get home and move on. I went to bed early that night. That was such a metaphor for how I was living. Can I just survive this "now" so that I can forget about it and move on? Can I just survive in this body? That night was no different. Later, I woke up with a start recognizing that this man was in my room. He was trying to kiss me and on top of me and I couldn't breathe. At first I thought, *Shit, I led him on.* I told him to stop and asked him to leave. I said I'm not interested in you in any way. Leave. And he did. I remember just wanting to get out of there. Just get me through the night. Just get me home. Then I went back to sleep praying for tomorrow. Well, tomorrow was worse, in fact it was one of the worst days of my life. He came back into my room later that night and would not take no for an answer. I fought him. I screamed at him. I even kicked him in the stomach and punched him in the face, but he was stronger. Then it was over and he left. I cried the rest of the night furious with my luck and enraged with a new, even deeper hatred than I thought was possible with my body. I waited until my friends woke up to call the police. Then I had a rape kit done, was questioned, and finally the highways were open and we went home.

Here is what I know now: I did not have a tattoo on my forehead saying, "Fuck me over." I was not empowered at that point in my life; that was true. But the assault was not my fault. It wasn't my fault and I didn't deserve it. It was life.

To this day I am certain that that man who assaulted me at the hotel was the catalyst in me beginning to save my own life. I was convinced at that point in my life that I was broken. I hated myself, my body, and my life. I loved my daughter and she got me out of bed every day, but I was so unhappy. I was the unhappiest that I'd ever been. I was going through the motions of my life, getting by, and praying for tomorrow. I wasn't living. I used to even say back then that I was half alive. I was alive but barely.

The police were not kind. My life at home once we got back felt like a nightmare. I wouldn't sleep. Anxiety followed me and became my shadow. But I was starting to wake up. It hurt. Life hurt. Waking up to my life hurt. Somehow though, trying to go back to sleep and continuing to walk through my life going through the motions hurt more. On some deep level I knew that the assault was not my fault but it did force me to see that I was still in an abuse cycle with my body and with my life. I was starting to see that there had to be more to life. This couldn't be all there was. I don't know how many months after that assault I cried myself to sleep every night. I was so scared. Even more than how scared I was about this man and the assault and being a single mom, I was terrified of my rage. I was pissed but could not and would not own or be with that. And what I did not understand at the time was that my body was holding onto and had absorbed the trauma and my emotional experience of the assault.

It wasn't my body's fault but my body was a constant reminder of what I wanted desperately to run from. Furthermore, it wasn't the trauma of the assault that was so painful. It was the stories that I was making up about me, my life, and my body based on what had happened that were excruciatingly painful. I couldn't run from it. I didn't want to breathe into or face it. But I also wanted to live. That assault was a catalyst for me finally reaching out to get help and support so that my life could change. I didn't know I would have to be the one to change my life, yet. I didn't know that I would be able to heal my past and my life. I didn't know that I would ever feel safe or free again but

I committed to finding a better way to live. That assault started the process of me getting intentional about creating more possibility for my life and for my daughter. I began growing up and growing through the darkness and shadows I was terrified to face. I brought my life out of the dark and began to see the light.

FIGHT FOR YOUR RIGHT TO LIVE

We are all leaders with life force in us. Anyone can find and live their dream with commitment and intention. What's not yours will fall away, making room for your greatest life story. We all want a great love story. What about living your greatest life story? It will include love, of course, but there is so much more. Love with another will never, ever, never, be enough to make your soul sing. You living as you, fully inspired, as you are, is the only magic potion that will make your soul sing. YOU are it. YOU are amazing. YOU can't be anyone other than who you really are, so what are you doing wasting time? I have thousands of shades of me, way more than fifty, and so do you. I prefer to let each shade shine as bright as possible, especially the ones that I can't stand. What about you? You tell me. You show me. You show the world now what's next. Let you out. You get to handle everything that shows up in your life your way. There's only your way. Anything else will feel like death. Anything else will be death. There is nothing worth that. There is nothing brave about killing ourselves off. Please don't let you die. Please, please let you live. Life's so precious. Your life is so precious. You are so precious. The only reason we stopped living is because our hearts got broken. To access possibility and life beyond the wall, we have to feel everything that we absolutely under no circumstances want to feel, or we are living as the walking dead.

GET BACK ON THE HORSE

There have been many moments in my life where the voice in my head told me that it would be easier just to quit. I have quit a lot. I have quit on my dreams. I have quit on my body. I have quit on lovers, friends, jobs, cities, states, and even some of my own family members. Luckily, this was just temporary insanity! I am not a quitter. My gut tells me that you are not a quitter either.

I think that people quit because they want to avoid pain and suffering. Makes sense, right? It's hard to argue with that. Let me argue anyway. Why not avoid pain and suffering at all costs? Because it means that you are not only admitting defeat but saying to the world, "I am not worthy or strong enough to handle this." The problem I see with this logic is that there is not anything that you have not survived. If you are reading this, then you are still here, committing to being the best that you can be.

You've already made it. Now is the time to begin to forgive and grow beyond your pain and your stories about what happened to you. What's next? What's now? Who will you be now? It wasn't your fault and now it's your work to move through and beyond that story and that worst-case scenario hell that you never wanted to have to face. You get to move forward. It won't work to try and turn a blind eye and pretend like it didn't happen or you weren't affected. You were. Because you are human and sensitive and gorgeous. You were impacted. We all have been impacted. But now we're all grown up. We're adults getting to choose moment to moment who we will be and what we will do. I know it happened and I know it hurt. It's time for you to get to experience new possibilities. It happened. It's over. It doesn't get to win. It's time for you to win. You get to win!

Another path to forgiving yourself is by acknowledging that your best is enough. We have enough time. Some of you may be thinking, *But I have wasted time.* That way of thinking and being is a., killing your soul, and b., keeping you in a holding pattern. You have enough time and you have lived every second of your life so far exactly how you did. We can't change that. You do get to look back on how you've lived and decide what you want to keep, remove and add, *from this moment forward.*

How do we take in fully the gorgeousness of life without experiencing parallels and paradoxes? The sun feels better after the snow melts. The snow is more beautiful and the rain and the wind once we've forgotten the magnificence of Mother Nature for a while. Stay committed and inspired even in the impossible and then life begins to flow. The sun doesn't come out all at once. You don't have to come into all of you in an instant either. Take your time. Your pace is perfection. You are perfection. You are a perfectly messy masterpiece. You get to come into who you really are fully. That is you in your greatness. And when people start to freak out and tell you how different you are, that's great. Even if it's not working for them, it means what you are doing is working.

Journal EXERCISE

- What is the wall in front of you now?

- What is your intention now for your life?

- What would you need to admit about yourself if you really could feel how you want to feel and create what you want to create, even though you've been hurt and been through so much already?

- What does it mean for your life that possibility really does exist for you, even if you've never seen it before, as long as you get intentional and committed?

- What is on the other side of the wall in front of you now?

- Grab that mirror again and look into your eyes and connect with the pain your body is holding. Your greatness lies underneath that pain; now connect to your greatness.

- Now acknowledge three of the moments where you were mean to yourself. Then say out loud, "I forgive me."

- Write yourself a forgiveness letter. Forgive yourself for your participation in avoiding conflict. Make a new commitment to honoring your internal guidance system.

Chapter Ten

THE AWAKENING

Life is not about the moments we want;
it's about the moments we have.

The new baby was not going to slow me down. I could still be superwoman, right? She-Ra was just another word for Rebeccah. I could be pregnant, a CEO, a coach, a wife, a mother, a daughter, a friend, a community leader, and a good citizen. Right? The sun was hot but I felt strong. My "Not Everything Stays in Vegas" T-shirt had me covered and confident that day. Sedona, Arizona is a magical place and I wanted some of its magic and I wanted my baby to have some of its magic. For several years I had been to Sedona to be part of training and graduating Integrative Holistic Life Coaches. Seven months pregnant or not, I was not going to miss that year's graduation. And my husband was a student graduating that year. We took the graduates on a hike and I was totally up for it, chock full of ego and pride, I was ready to show everyone what I was made of.

I was like *The Little Engine That Could* on steroids. I wouldn't be stopped by anything. It was all about me. The hike got harder but I was doing great. That is until the facilitator, my coach and trainer for years, suddenly yelled "Stop!" We had gotten to a section of the hike where there were two boulders that you had to shimmy through to get to the next leg of the hike. There were no foot or hand holds. I wasn't scared. Then I realized that she was yelling at *me* to stop. She asked me if I had thought about what the risks were. Coming down I would have to face forward as I shimmied down. What if I fell? What about the baby? What about my husband? I was furious. Breathing fire furious. Not my proudest moment but it was a "full of fear, unexpressed anger and grief, pride and ego" moment that ended up changing my life forever. It was the beginning of another new level of life and awakening.

After some conversation, consideration, and realizations about how self-absorbed I was being, I looked into my husband's eyes. I hadn't raised a baby with anyone before. My oldest likes to call us the "Gilmore Girls." It was her and I against the world and my calls were the only calls. This was different. *I* was different. I was with a man who told me constantly that he wanted a family, with me, and he genuinely wanted to be a father. On the side of that mountain, I started to see so much that I was still carrying emotionally. Shame. A commitment to pushing men away. Not trusting that I was supported. Not wanting to be seen as weak. Beliefs about doing it alone, not being able to have business, and a family, and myself all at the same time, my husband would never stick around, the list goes on. The group was willing to support me in safely getting up that mountain but I decided to sit there, right where I was, keeping my baby safe, myself safe, and I cried.

My tears ran rivers down that mountain. More people than I could have ever counted stopped to check on the crazy, very pregnant woman, losing it. But I was okay. I was waking up to the fact that I was actually going to have this baby, committed to partnership with her father. I was seeing my self-absorption and willingness to risk the baby, my marriage, and myself.

I cried for at least two hours waiting for the group to come back. I sat by a tree and let it all out. The grief, anger, fear, joy, and excitement that all flowed out of me that day had me lighter and more aware than ever that day afterward.

The relief on my husband's face as the group came back to get me was so beautiful. I decided to take in his love, and the baby, and give up the all-about-me way that I had been living during that pregnancy. We were in this together.

The next week I was diagnosed with cancer. That hike was the beginning of me meeting me and cutting out the emotional cancer in my life that I had control over. My favorite part about this story is that where I was sitting stubborn and having my tantrum, was a vortex. A vortex is an energy field where the theory is that miraculous healing occurs. I had wanted desperately to get to the top of that mountain because that's where I thought the vortex was. Vortices are energy centers that promote healing and connection, and I wanted that baby in the vortex. Turns out where God had me sit my ass down to get my shit together was the vortex.

We carry heaviness and emotional cancer that isn't ours to carry. Any place that we are committed to disrespecting life, whether we meant to or not, has us toxic. Any place where we're dimming down, dumbing down, or selling out is making us toxic. Any place where we worry about "supposed to's" is toxic. Any place where we cave on our truth is making us toxic. Over-functioning is making us toxic. Our addiction to feeling unworthy and living in spite of our pasts and our mistakes is making us toxic. Trying to fit in, attempting to impress and prove our worthiness is making us toxic. Hating on our bodies is making us toxic.

LISTEN TO WHISPERS OR
THEY WILL BECOME SCREAMS

Your life will talk to you. It will scream when you won't listen. It knows what is and is not serving you. It's communicating with you always. When we ignore, dismiss, or reject the whispers and signals life is sending our way, they get louder. Pain means that we weren't listening to the whispers. We didn't pay enough attention. Life knows and it will talk and it wants to honor you and carry you safely and comfortably through your life. It wants to serve you and it is serving you. It wants you to get the most out of your life. We just stopped listening. The whispers can be subtle, like a light breeze that you almost don't even notice. Your headache was just some tension in your neck at one time. Your back pain got more intense when you kept pushing. Hear this, life is going to give you a clear spiritual YES or NO with every option that will ever show up in front of you. Go slower. Breathe deeper into your body which is the house of your soul and your truth and listen.

The good news is that no one can determine or advise you on the next right step for you, but your soul and your life will give you signals as to what does and does not feel right, for you. Feel into your soul when you feel stuck, scared, or don't know. It can and will guide you. You can find inspiration to take on your life. Our bodies and lives want us to be relaxed and flowing, but when we fight so hard against life the way it is and our inner guidance system, we struggle a lot. That perfect soul that is you is constantly striking up a conversation with you and any time you listen and engage you will receive a crystal clear "Yes, please" or a "No, thank you." This is true whatever it is that you are facing or up against in your life, and your choices can always land on the "Yes, please" when you are awake and aware.

SELF-CARE STARTS ON THE INSIDE

You've got to be the one to create your self-care plan. No matter what you've done, or have been through or are afraid of, you deserve to feel incredible and you deserve self-care. This whole self-care thing though is not cookie cutter. Healing isn't cookie cutter. And no professional knows better for you than you do if you are really paying attention. I have a hard ask for you. I'm asking you to get on that horse and ride it into the dawn of your new beginning with your experience of emotional self-care. How it's been isn't how it has to be. How it was was your best then but if you've made it this far in this book you know too much now to go back to how you've been living in (not) caring for yourself. I'm not suggesting that you throw everything out, just get really honest. Eliminate the shoulds. Before cancer, self-care was just an afterthought for me.

I started slowly reinventing my self-care plan after cancer and the baby. It was yoga, baths, reading, healthy food, an incredible holistic medical team, sleep, sex the way I needed it, lots of sleep and water, and that was all I could do. Then I could walk, then bike, then hike, and now I strength train. I have slowly added in what feels good and honors me. This was painful for a while because I was hell bent on comparing what I thought that I should be doing for self-care with what the industry or people I wanted to emulate were suggesting, but my body wasn't there, yet. And other people's road maps and models were not right for my life. Now I listen to me and guide my self-care plan. I am the CEO of my self-care and you are the CEO of yours. Honor that and take self-care on from a new place of awareness that includes emotional self-care.

What's your passion? Add it to your self-care plan. Maybe you write, or draw, or play sports, or love movies—add it in. Add dates and adventure. I have a date night with my sexy husband every single week. And weekly dates with my kids, separately. It's all self-care and I hope that you are noticing that self-care is so much more than food, water, and exercise. Know your preferences and honor your body and your life your way. That's what self-care is! It can look like: feeling through your emotions, positive self-talk, hobbies/fun, personal growth/coach/seminars/education, reading, water, nutrition, routines, social life, family time, sleep, sex, travel, baths, adventure, and so much more.

HEALING IS AN INSIDE JOB

Healing and coming back to life creates movement and momentum. Movement is what will heal you, one breath at a time. One moment at a time. Ask yourself, *Who will I be now? What would heal me the most now?* Another level of healing and self-care is diving into our failures, regrets, and deepest wounds. Let's go here. I promise you can handle it. What is your greatest failure? Do you know? One at a time, it's time to pull out and look at the thorns in your side that poked holes in your soul. If you let this overwhelm you, it can. Or you can consider that this exploration of where it hurts the most is what will guarantee that you get your life back—and more life.

This is how your light gets out. Life will poke you and poke you and poke you and poke you. You haven't peaked. Start now, from where you are. It's not the end. I am screaming at you, to go, grow, live, ready or not, now! Let's go live. You will never be ready. Just breathe and choose consciously what it is in this moment that you are going to breathe into. When all else fails, breathe into you, in your body and into your life. You are the only one who can. Get it wrong? You will. You will fail, a lot. So what? Let's stop living on autopilot. Let's stop selling out and giving ourselves away for any reason.

I felt crazy for so many years when I began working with coaches, participating in seminars, and on volunteer support teams supporting seminars, because I refused to not take responsibility for my wounds, my experience and my impact. I knew it was never other people or the situation at hand that was upsetting me and I wanted to be free. Every trigger led to another layer of freedom, but I felt crazy and alone and very misunderstood most of the time. It worked though. And I can't thank every gorgeous person who watched and loved me through the falling apart of my survival personality and the dying of my ego. I will tell you the work of awareness and self-responsibility is the answer. So many days I felt like I was going to die if I dealt with all of this shit that was clogging up my life. But I knew, somehow, deep down, that if I didn't do the work to clean up my life then I would miss my life.

The hardest part for me was recognizing where I had impacted others in a negative way. I knew that my intentions were good but even with the best intentions when we are asleep and still living in survival mode, we can't see our negative ripple. I asked to see so I saw. I asked everyone I was working with to tell me the truth about how they were experiencing me, how I hurt them, and how I could be better. I asked how I had impacted them. I asked to hear their experience of me and I asked them to tell me exactly what I had done or not done that was hurtful, not useful, or not working.

My work in participating in hundreds of seminars helped me become who I wanted to be. It was an overhaul that required me to be fully vulnerable. I learned how to forgive everything about life, me, my past, the world, but most of all I learned how to forgive the humanity in me and the humanity in others because I now understand so clearly where it all comes from. I had to get defensive, blaming, hysterical, and forgive myself for it. I had to face all of my worst fears and my dark side. I had to forgive myself for being so comfort-able in the dark, surviving my way through life, and from there I had to forgive myself for pushing love and life away.

And then I had reinvention work to do. With everyone I had impacted, not just with the people that I thought deserved it. You see if other people are never the problem in terms of how I am feeling and how I am experiencing life, then they are all teachers. All people reflect how I feel about me and life back to me. Same is true for you. I choose to see people as innocent. I am going to ask you to try this on as well. I don't think we want to hurt each other. I think we feel powerless and try to take our power back without realizing the impact that has on other people. As I've said, I also think we are fighting with ghosts. We project the people that we never healed with onto the people in our lives now. We can't actually see the people in front of us in their greatness and in their innocence when we're unaware and still playing out our pain. There is a better way. It's unconventional. It's not easy. But it does exist. The world will help you defend your bad behavior and your upsets, but is it really worth it?

We've spent enough of our precious lives uncomfortable in our own skin, blaming and being less of who we are. It's been normal to white-knuckle our way through fear as we kill our spirits off, in a state of sheer loathing for life. Shivers of self-doubt and self-hatred have gone through us like lightning. Escaping how we genuinely feel has been the goal for many, and for most of their lives. How many min-utes have we tried to wish away our lives, our emotions, our bodies, our beauty, and our magnificence? Your life is beyond magnificent. No matter how much you've wished yourself away, you stayed intact, whole, and perfect in all of your flaws.

YOUR FLAWS ARE THE FROSTING

If you are lucky enough to know my flaws that means I have let you in. If I have the honor of knowing about your flaws, how blessed am I? You in your humanity is beyond gorgeous. Not wanting to embrace, accept, or live as who we really are is the greatest shame possible. Twelve surgeries and four months of chemotherapy later, I *got it.* There was never a thing wrong with my perfect, perfect, perfect body. Perfection lies in seeing the magic of what it is that is now, in front of us, that's not going anywhere until we handle it. Instead of striving to be perfect or for perfection from others and the world, see the perfection life offers exactly as it feels and exactly how it is in the moment you're in. Yes, I am asking a lot of you. Yes, I am asking for you to up your game—a lot. Yes, I am asking you to get more present in the exact moments that you want to fight, run away from, or resist. Resistance is futile and empty. I'm asking you to make it your job to handle you, how you are being and who you are being. We are not separate from each other. Your mind, your body, your spirit, they are just as important, special and significant as mine and as any living breathing life. We all have hopes and dreams. What would life be like if you went to bed knowing you were clean, meaning your best was and is enough, and you're off the hook? The only thing we can do is know we've done our best and commit to better next time if needed. It's enough. It really is.

If we won't get clean and clear emotionally, then we take our woundedness out on our kids, our lovers, the people around us, and on the world. You are not over. You are still here. I know you've been hurt by people, life, words, and there have been blindsides. I'm not giving people who behaved badly a free pass or saying it didn't happen. It's not okay what happened but it doesn't have to stop you anymore. Who will you be now? You've made it this far. What can you create, become, and accomplish from a place of total freedom and being fully alive? It's not the world or people that have broken you down, and I know you've been hurt. It's you resigning that hurts more than anything. I'm offering you a way to take full control over your relationship with your entire life so that you can take your life back. You don't have to do any of this but I promise that you can. Resignation is the death of your soul. You are more than your apathy. You can thrive regardless of circumstances. The key is awareness. You choose what you are committed to now. Will you continue to commit to a life of "It hurts too much but it's what I know," or will you be brave enough to commit to a life that you love and that inspires you?

FROM THIS MOMENT FORWARD BE VULNERABLE IN LOVE, NOT SAFETY

All of this I hope is piquing your interest and sounds appealing. But how do you clear up, repair, and reinvent—with people? How do you make relationships stronger? Understand that the goal isn't to be received well. One of three things will happen as you lead in loving vulnerability, committed to being your best for humanity and every life in front of you. First, they will easily work with you, work it out, and grow with you. The second thing that can happen is people get triggered and get over it, do their work, and grow with you. The third is they go away. Let them go. Instead of avoiding the conflict I'm asking you to be brave and hold space for it. Conflict can bring you closer, if you'll let it. When other people are upset, making yourself responsible for their emotions is pointless. You didn't do anything to cause them to feel how they feel and they didn't do anything to cause you to feel how you feel either. This is hard to grasp but I promise it's the truth. The patterns you have with people don't happen because of the person; they happen because you still haven't healed that emotional wound.

Think about how many unhealed people there are. So many are walking around all clogged up and heartbroken, reinforcing their wounds and insecurities, begging to be loved. Let's leap you even more now. Consider that it's another level of commitment to a breakthrough life when you get willing to listen to people and get willing to hear what they have to say about their upset and how you may have contributed. You can know your best was enough and take the feedback from life and other people to see where you can grow even more or become even more of who you want to be. It's delicate because you aren't responsible for other people or the experience of life that they are having or how they feel. However, they can help you see sides of yourself that you didn't even know were there. Remember, it's not your fault, but it is your work. They are sharing with you a pattern and an experience that haunts them. When you are strong enough and vulnerable enough to connect to them, while they are in their experience as the best of you in that moment, it's healing for you both. It's easy to write people off but once again, the patterns—like abandonment, rejection, feeling too much, feeling misunderstood, competition, guilt, and shame—continue.

When someone is upset, as long as they are respectful and not projecting onto you, ask them to tell you more. Lean in. Have a bring-it-on attitude when conflict shows up in you and in your relationships, as you commit to a breakthrough life for you, no matter what they say or do or have done. For the healing to really happen there has to be a new solution. I've learned the art of negotiating as long as it takes until there is a win/win solution. This is different from a compromise.

Only agree to what you know would bring you closer together and what you know will really work for you. It's also so important to communicate without blame, threat, or intimidation, and with an open heart. I recommend asking permission before attempting a difficult conversation. Ask when a good time would be to talk or sit down face to face. Let them know how much you care about them and the relationship and that your intention is to get more connected and into a better place when and if they are ready and willing. Then I suggest a ground rule of respect. Listen. Speak about you and your experience with no defensiveness, blame, threat, intimidation or manipulation. If you need a break, ask for that. If they ask for a break that's okay. In my experience, showing up for the difficult conversations gives a lot of very important information. Know you had the conversation. It will either bring more connection and healing or show you that this relationship is part of your past and not part of your future.

The big point here is that other people can't harm or threaten you when you stop taking responsibility for their experience and stop making you responsible for their experience. You can see where you could do better next time, acknowledge that, apologize and ask them if there is anything you can do now—but that's really it. The rest is up to them.

Now, you may be wondering, what about people who are so toxic it would be foolish or dangerous to try and have or continue a relationship with? I am not asking you to step into a lion's den. I am saying that as long as the person in front of you is not physically, emotionally, or mentally abusive, try this out. If they are abusive or have a history of being abusive set some ground rules. Let them know you want to talk as long as the conversation remains healthy and respectful. Now, if the person is just so abusive that you would be putting yourself at risk to attempt a conversation, you could try a phone call or just write a letter in a notebook that you choose maybe to give them—but maybe not. Again, the game is ultimately you with you. The healing is absolutely for you. And remember, there's no right way or wrong way to live your life or to relate to others. There's just what works for you. What I am certain of, is if a particular relationship is keeping you up at night or on your mind in a way that is stressful or upsetting, you have healing work to take on with them or at the very least within yourself. And being brave enough to face and do that work is so incredibly freeing. They don't get to have power over you and your life. Emotional clearing work in relationships is miraculous. So often the relationship can heal and reinvent beautifully. And when that's not the case at least you can get to a place where you genuinely healed your heart, seeing them as innocent, and yourself as innocent, knowing what takes care of you now.

Back to that third thing that can happen when you are aware and responsibly leading in being "clean" in your relationships, the person goes away. We can't force other people to want to work it out with us. We can't make them want to be a part of our lives. My theory is that the people who are aligned with your vibe will always work it out and grow with you, even if the process is hard, painful, or uncomfortable. The key is for you to know that you did everything you could. Then it's no longer up to you. What is up to you is whether or not you keep your heart open and whether or not you are available for healing and growing with them if they do choose to come back wanting that too. I think when people go away it's because they are on a different path. It's not personal and there is nothing you can do to stop it. People who go away are looking for something different than you are. Let them go in love with an open heart. Don't let it make you harder.

LEAVE YOUR HEART OPEN

People will either work with you, get mad and get over it and work with you, or go away. Regardless, when you keep your heart open, this keeps you clean with yourself and lets you live a fuller life, and feel more alive. It's so easy when we get confronted, triggered, heartbroken or get our feelings hurt to want to put our guard up, and to wrap armor around our hearts. The problem with that is when you're guarded, you also prevent life and love from getting in. And guardedness, quite honestly, creates more unnecessary toxicity, disease, and suffering. For many, the default setting has been a defensive posture, of guarding and protecting ourselves. That pushes love and life away. I'm asking you to consider flirting with the possibility of letting your guard down and leaving your heart open. There are a few reasons why I think this is super beneficial to you and your life.

I'm not saying pretend that everything that's happening is a gift or it's good, and you just can't see it yet. That's not what I'm saying. I don't believe in positivity or that it's all a gift. I believe in possibility. You can use what's happening in life to let yourself be more of who you are. To let yourself open your heart more so that you can love yourself more, in the moment, and let more life and experience in. I'm asking you to love as much as you could and can in this lifetime. What would that be like to know? No matter what, people are going to come, people are going to go, but you can absolutely know that you lived and loved as much as you could.

At the end of the day, when your head hits the pillow, ask yourself, *Did I let love in today? Did I keep my heart open?* This is like *the ultimate fountain of youth,* in my opinion. The more you're willing to love and lead and be walking around with your heart open, energetically, you're spreading a possibility that will help us all heal.

Healing is possible. I do believe that it starts with you. And what if we could, each of us, start to become a catalyst for a new normal, where instead of defending, guarding our hearts and loving less, we love more instead with an open heart. Because honestly, in this society, we are willing to love less way too much of the time. I want us to be willing to love more, especially when it's hard.

What if it's possible to become an emotionally healed adult? It is our own behaviors, choices, and meltdowns that create toxic relationship dynamics. It's never the other person's fault. People are never inherently bad. They fall into toxic dynamics with themselves and others and that is when things start to fall apart. All relationships can show us more about the relationship that we have with ourselves, which is the only one we can work on. You see other people through your filter of what you are used to experiencing in relationships. Make a commitment to have a new experience because you refuse to go toxic. Instead of needing other people to change, step into a willingness to face, move through, and conquer whatever conflicts show up, in you, in them, in life, and in the relationship, and you can be free.

If you are in danger, by all means get safe, get help, and get out. If you are upset, dig deeper. I'm going to focus on upsets and how they can ruin relationships. It's tragic that one conversation, one choice, or one moment where feelings got hurt can destroy a relationship in a flash. Contrary to what we are taught, toxic relationships are never the other person's fault. And conflicts can actually make relationships stronger and more connected. Find your part in the breakdowns. Do better even if they won't. It will change all of your relationships. Consider that people do their best. See them as innocent and doing their best, even if you think they don't deserve it. People get upset, get mean, shut down, the list goes on. However, when you are your best self, there is a lot more room to hold space with an open heart for people when they are having a moment. It's when you are running on fumes, depleted, and drained that the chances of relationship drama increase, fast.

All relationships can heal, repair and reinvent if both people are willing to be respectful, loving and care about being their best for the other. When you are drained, not liking you in the relationship, or needing the other person to be different for you to be okay, you are in trouble. We need to not be so afraid of conflict in our relationships. Relationships can hold us to higher standards, to our own standards, when we let them. You being different in the relationship can heal the relationship and your relationship patterns. If you wait for the other person to change, you stay in your patterns and from there you will keep re-experiencing the same patterns with new people over and over again. Many people pick and choose who they will be their best with instead of treating all people and all relationships like they matter. Don't lie, withhold, or pretend that you are okay when you are not. No settling. No compromise. No dumbing it down. Treat every life in front of you like that person is worth you being your best for them because they are. All relationships deserve you being your best with an open heart, no matter what, starting with the one with yourself.

MAKE ROOM FOR MIRACLES

Leave your heart open. I know you'll be glad you did . . . eventually, if not now. I'm glad that I leave my heart open when I do, because what happens is I make room for miracles. When I won't do that, when I'm shut down, when I'm guarded, when I'm right about my triggers, when I'm convincing myself that somebody else caused my upset or a situation, there's not a lot of life happening in that moment.

It's not easy, but it is a new habit that you can nurture and cultivate as a new muscle to build, explore, and experiment with. When we're building muscles, it doesn't always feel comfortable. Sometimes they hurt, but that doesn't mean you stop working on strengthening and developing muscles. I don't think there's anything to do other than keep our hearts open. And I see people pushing each other away every single day. You don't need more time to heal. You don't need more time to be right about your issues. Leave your heart open and let yourself love and experience life, regardless of what's happening outside of you, regardless of what other people are doing. That's freedom.

Let your mission of living fully become your reality. Be brave enough to stop and let go of anything that isn't supporting your mission.

BEWARE: PEOPLE WON'T GET IT

And that's not a reason to hold you back and distance yourself from your body and soul. Commit to the life you want, no matter what life looks like now, aware that you are free. You are the only source of freedom that you will ever have. As adults and powerful humans, we don't *have* to settle; we *choose* to settle. It makes us sick and miserable when we settle for a mediocre life. I've never met anyone who wanted a mediocre life. What I mean by a mediocre life is a tolerating what we don't really want. I'm not saying that there are better lives or ways to live than others. What I'm saying—*again*—is that the life of your dreams is yours for the taking. You are driving now.

Awareness is not an "as long as" process. It's a way of living. None of us will be perfect but we can wake up, faster and faster. Now you know you can give yourself permission to prioritize yourself, your lives, and how you want to feel. We now know not to let the spiritual gas that keeps us full of energy and life force run out. No more taking on the weight of what we can't control. Now we are aware and already better for everyone.

BOUNDARIES OR BLURRED LINES

Boundaries are not walls. They hold you as you grow into new and more expansive life and possibility. Now let's take awareness a step further and talk about not only keeping your heart open, but keeping your heart open while you set, have, and honor clear boundaries. Boundaries allow you to hold the possibility that you want for yourself and for your life. First, where do you want your life to go? Next, what do you need to stay solid within yourself and to stay committed to that vision? That's what boundaries offer us. They're not you trying to get other people to change. They are for you.

Boundaries hold the life you have now while you build the life you want. They allow you to stay on track knowing what you will do when life goes against your boundaries. They help you stay awake and aware of what you won't engage in and what you will engage in. Another great question is, "What alignment needs to occur in me to be able to do what I'm doing and go where I'm going, regardless of what's happening around me?" Nobody ever got closer to the life they wanted by having poor or no boundaries. We need to make the boundaries we've committed to happen, regardless of the show called life and the world and other people. The show is going to be the show. Welcome to being alive. Boundaries keep you on point and on course.

LET IT FALL APART

Cancer was a spiritual crisis. Cancer had me up my awareness game, big time. It felt like I was dying emotionally and spiritually—and

I was. Thank God. It was terrible, not knowing who I was. The fear of the unknown. The questioning was endless. I questioned everything. I questioned who I was. What I believed. What I thought about everything I had learned. Me as a coach. Me as a mother. Me as a daughter, friend, me as a wife. Me as a woman. My spirituality shattered around me like a favorite vase falling off a shelf. It was from that place of being shattered on every level that I realized that life isn't about the moments we want. It's about the moments we have. I decided to live like I was going to live, aware of the pain. Aware of how delicate life is. Aware of my broken heart. Aware of my strength and ability to listen to what I believed would keep me alive as the active leader of my healing. I didn't do it alone. And I was calling the shots for the first time in my life.

My coach and I had a coaching call and we talked about chemo. I already knew I had an unrelated benign brain tumor that could grow and become dangerous. I already knew that surgeons had gotten all of the cancer that they could see, and that the chemo was meant to kill off any cancer cells that were microscopic and in my blood. I also knew that I was dying. My right leg was dying as the nerves that went down that leg into my foot were dying. I was suicidal. The chemo had a side effect of suicidal ideation that was real, loud, and *terrifying.* I couldn't listen to the chemical voices in my head, or the pain, and *live.* It was one or the other. I was at the ultimate fork in the road of my life. My coach and I worked through my fear of quitting chemo when the truth was that my inner guidance was saying, Quit or you will die. It became clear that it was time to stop the chemo and it became clear how loved and supported I was. Boundaries were tricky here because my doctors and even some family members were not seeing what I was seeing or in agreement with my choices. I held steady with my boundaries of what I would do, what I wouldn't do, and honored myself and my life. I trusted myself, finally. It was then that I took the helm of the ship called my life and I led. It *worked.*

GET SUPPORT

Believe it or not you are supported right now in everything you are doing. Have your support system set up to support *who you really are* and your highest self. I am going to challenge you to get rid of what supports and strokes where you've been asleep and unhealed. Face the music. Get blissfully happy. Live your healthiest life by staying awake and aware. If you are reading then you are still here, as the best that you can be. Life gets easier once you wake up. Keep going through the growing pains, awake and aware, with an open heart, with boundaries, and with support, and you have the beginning of blissful happiness.

Journal EXERCISE

- What does awareness mean to you now?

- How will you know when you are aware? What will you do when you notice that you've fallen asleep temporarily? How will you bring awareness back?

- How will you keep your heart open?

- Who are three people that you know with whom you need to clear up things?

- What would it be like to know you loved as much as you could in your lifetime?

- Create a list of who is in your inner circle, i.e., the people who support you and are following you.

- Ask your inner circle to give you honest feedback about how they experience you. Receive the feedback.

Chapter Eleven

THE MIRACLES

What if everything you saw, touched, heard, desired, tasted, and wanted was a miracle simply waiting for you to make eye contact with it?

I was in another seminar, in the woods. I was supposed to be (or at least I thought that we were supposed to be) at a different location. We had gone hiking and just as in life, the plans had changed and I was now in the woods and it looked like we were going to be there for a while. I'm pregnant. It's raining. I have no supplies. Honestly, I'm miserable. The poncho I have on doesn't protect me from the cold and now I have to pee. I find a spot and I'm thinking, *I'm pregnant, wearing a poncho, peeing in the rain, in the woods, and I have no clue what's going on.* Laughter erupts out of the depths of me. Giggles turn into a belly laugh. Now I'm talking out loud to myself and to the baby: "We're not alone. This is not my favorite circumstance that I've ever been in, but we're okay."

As my thoughts wander, with a smile on my face, I look at the water and the trees. It's really beautiful. It occurs to me that I've been working so much, for so many years, that I stopped getting outside and connecting to nature. For a moment it feels like going back to the cornfields of my childhood. I'm outside and it's miraculous. I connect to a playful side of myself that's been shut down for a long, long time. Why not make this a game? I decide to soak up being in nature as I reconnect to my roots. Music starts to escape my lips, as I walk to the water singing, uninhibited. I used to sing opera but it's been years. I love to sing. I used to sing almost daily. What happened? Why had I stopped?

This moment becomes pivotal as I start to believe that whatever life throws at me, I can get to a place of neutrality. I don't have to like or love, or even prefer a circumstance to be able to live in healed leadership through that experience. *Whoa.* I can feel my body as it holds me and the baby. I listen as my soul continues to talk. At first, it's a tiny whisper, telling me, *Feel the breeze. Sleep under the stars. I've got you. The rain will end. The sun will come out. I've got you. Sit by the water and discover you, in this magnificent body, in the deliciousness of this day, in your most beautiful life.* I listen. And then the sun does come out. This is the moment that I realize that I can be in a situation that's not my preference, get to neutral, find my bearings, and powerfully choose.

CREATE YOUR COMEBACK STORY

That seminar was one month before the seminar where I was still pregnant, on the hike in Sedona. Back to back, right before the cancer diagnosis, I received much needed foreshadowing and spiritual direction to prepare me for what was to come. This was all preparation for my comeback story. What if it's *all* preparing us?

Not some of it, all of it, even when it feels the worst? Your relationship with your life is not going to change overnight. How you have been living, what you have been living with and carrying, and letting it go to make room for more *is possible*. It has hurt like hell but it doesn't have to anymore. There will be plenty of moments where it might feel easier and more attractive to stick your head in the sand or into a bowl of ice cream, but just keep breathing and visualize life without the heaviness that you feel. Make it a game. Make it the exact preparation that you've been needing to create your comeback story.

What happened in those woods over the course of three days was me getting grounded and rooted. Trees that are so deeply rooted into the earth that they can't be moved during storms are the trees that survive the storm. We all have the ability to get more rooted. We resist grounding because then we'd have to feel. By now I hope that you can see that feeling it all, rooted in your strength and essence, is the key to getting and experiencing as much life as possible. In fact, it's when we're not rooted and grounded that we're the most at risk. We can't see things coming when we're going through the motions. We can see so much more coming when we're grounded in who we choose to be.

Honor all that life has given you. You're a force to be reckoned with. You may feel bored or even wrecked now but you can rebuild and renew your relationship with your life. You are stronger than your pain and your past. Your life is perfect for you. How do I know? Because it's the life you have. Your circumstances aren't you but your life is housing you and keeping you alive and well through every breath and every moment. You get to choose your next steps now. You get to change your life starting with how you relate to and honor it. What I want you to know is that your life is worth living for. *You are worth living for.* Your life is giving you all it can. Your dream life is yours for the taking. No more waiting. No more wishing. Lead, fully alive, so that you can become fully live.

THE AWAKENING

Look forward. The past is over and you will get to a point where it no longer haunts you, so that the painful experience you've been having and reliving over and over again, truly is over. What happened still happened but the life you're choosing to live now and the future that you are looking forward to is more powerful. Listen to life's whispers. Your life will talk to you. It will scream when you won't listen and are focused on looking backward. It knows what is and is not serving you. It's communicating with you always. When we ignore, dismiss, or reject life's signals, they get louder. Your life wants to honor you and carry you safely and comfortably through all of your seasons. Our world itself has an opportunity to come together with a shared vision that supports people with reinvention and healing after a global pandemic. Now is the perfect time to break through anything that's in the way of living a happy and healthy life, and from there we can help each other.

Every day brings opportunity for drama. In my house there are dozens of moments, every day, where I could easily engage in family feuding, fighting, or guarding of my heart. But my favorite part about my little family is we talk through and have the hard conversations when needed. And we do keep our hearts open. Life isn't a game that any of us can be perfect at. I'm not perfect, but I'm trying to model leaving my heart open, being willing to let love and life in, even if I'm scared or hurting or upset. And I want that for my kids as well. My husband and I have had epic fights. We are not the perfect couple. And when we fight we do so for connection, reinvention, and growth, and we leave our hearts open. I'm so grateful to have a spouse who is willing to leave his heart open as I also leave mine open and from there we get through it all, together. My husband, daughters, and I have created our comeback story. We could have easily surrendered into the depths of despair and given ourselves permission to be our worst, instead of our best. But we didn't. The family I've been a part of creating and nurturing is part of my comeback story. This book is part of my comeback story. What will you create in your comeback story? You get to have one and I cannot wait to hear all about it.

THE MIRACLE IS YOU

Once you give yourself permission to fall in love with your life, your whole life can become a blast. You are supposed to have fun. You are meant to receive all the good that life has to offer you. You are supported. You are deserving. You are worthy. You are a miracle. You are free. Life is meant to feel free. You are meant to be free. Your life is happening now. Your life is carrying you now. You don't need an escape, or to wait until tomorrow, or for life to be different than it is. *You are home.*

You've got to have hope to begin. Hope isn't enough, but it's a start. My hope is that this book brings you hope. From there you've got to pay attention to your life more than ever. Please know how beautiful you are and have always been. Your entire life has never been anything less than beautiful. When you feel yourself starting to lose hope, look into your eyes and see your substance and depth. Your life, every second of it, has mattered and made a difference. I honor you.

Life is a complicated masterpiece but your relationship with it does not have to be complicated. It's simple. Choose how you treat yourself, choose how you want to live and who you want to be, and everything will start to change. That's the scary and fantastic part. I know it may seem like if everything starts to change you'll lose you or the life you have now. The losses make room for trading up. You get to upgrade your relationship with your life. What goes away as a result was dead weight. Sluff it off. Brush yourself off. Pick yourself up. Keep breathing.

You will need support. Don't think you will be successful with your comeback story going Lone Ranger. When you grow, your support needs to grow with you. Some will get it. Some won't. Don't let that discourage you or take you off course. It's not about who is going to support you. It's about what type of support you want and need. It may be nutrition. It may be childcare. It may be accountability or an assistant. Whatever it is, once you know what you need and ask for it, your life force will support you in reaching your goal. Remember, if you know what you don't want, then you know what you want, including support. What hasn't worked in the past won't work now either. Try something new. Keep going until you start to feel momentum. The only thing you can truly lose is you. Don't you dare let that happen! You will hit walls. You'll want to quit—just don't! If it's a dead end, turn around. Don't deny yourself the privilege of being who you are every day, while you take on your ultimate relationship with your life so that you can *have* the ultimate life that you've been wishing and longing for.

My wish is that after reading this book you let yourself get what you want most. Believe me you do know what you want most. It's just been covered up and maybe there was a point when you decided there were more reasons why you can't have what you want than reasons why you can. Change your mind. We are each responsible for getting and creating what we want most. We wait because it didn't happen or come through in our childhoods. Be the person now that comes through for you. Your life will take it from there and it will take you all the way home.

For so long I thought I couldn't survive rejection. But what I didn't realize was that I was rejecting myself day after day after day, not letting myself connect with and live into the life I wanted to live. Everything about my life changed when I decided that my life mattered and I'm supposed to be here on the planet, getting the most out of my life, healed and making my difference. I'm not hurting anyone living out loud and fully vibrant, and neither will you. Inspiration is a commitment to being you in any and every moment. It's about being willing to be with and lead from whatever life dishes out. Life is unpredictable and beautiful, and sometimes we don't get what we want, how we want it. Just because something doesn't go your way, yet, doesn't mean that the magic and miracles aren't waiting for you right around the corner. Life isn't about you becoming whole. You're already whole. Miracles are only as available to you as your willingness to move through *and* heal through your deepest fears. A miracle is when you know on the deepest possible level that everything is okay, working out, and that you and your life are better than okay. Miracles are there even in tragedy. Miracles happen when we grow through our blocks to love and life.

There is where we are and there is always another side. We want to skip the middle. The middle is the part where you have to get through what's in the way of where you want to be. The middle is the gold. The middle is what gives you access to the miracles. And if you don't get through the middle, you miss the miracle and go back to the beginning. Where you are now and where you want to be are separate because of your blocks and your fear. Your perception, however, is why there is a gap between where you want to be and where you are. Once your perception becomes a new, profound commitment to being who it takes to experience a miracle, you're there. Home run! Your patterns and blocks begin and end in a moment. It's your beliefs about what's happening and your commitment to your story about what is happening that is keeping you stuck and far away from seeing the miracle that's right there, hidden in plain sight.

We get caught up in a moment like it's absolute. Moments are just moments. They come and they go but you and your life remain. Breathe and align. That's all there is to do. You are it. The answer has always been you. You are the miracle. Your life is a miracle. When all else fails for me, I have a personal practice of praying for a miracle. When I feel the storm coming or find myself in the middle of the storm I surrender and say, *I'm praying for a miracle. Please show me the miracle.* Inevitably, like the sun rising again, miracles reveal themselves. Because I asked for it. Because I committed to being who it takes to realizing the miracles waiting for me, and I fall into them.

CONQUER THE MOUNTAIN

I'm often asked what got me through cancer. I'll tell you. Miracles. I knew that I couldn't control cancer. It was going to take me out or I was going to make it and none of it would be up to me. A miracle. What I knew I could control was how I played the game called cancer. A miracle. I was a natural disaster of emotions. I would scream when I needed to scream and cry when I needed to cry. I'd shake when it was time to let my hands and my voice shake. A miracle. What I decided, and honestly I am not sure why, was that cancer was going to be what allowed me to meet myself in this lifetime. And it was. It was the ultimate seminar. It was a time when I got to meet myself and see what I'm made of. A miracle. My biggest life question came when it was time to ask myself, *Do you know who you are when you are thirty-four and pregnant with a family and a business and a life that you really, really, really want to live fully?* I didn't. I decided I would find out. A miracle. That's what got me through. I knew that I couldn't heal cancer but I knew that I was more powerful. A miracle.

I decided that cancer and I were going to have to learn how to get along. This was the beginning of a major turning point for me with my relationship with my life. A miracle. I was starting to see the forest through the trees. It became increasingly clear to me that cancer was going to be my teacher. I was going to see what I was truly made of. I had always wanted to get the most out of my life and now was my chance. A miracle. The fear was suffocating but I knew that I had to either commit to miracles or quit; there were no other options. A miracle. I was fearful that if I didn't commit to life that I would unravel so fast that I would never recover. A miracle. Spinning out was not the answer. I wanted in, not out of my life. A miracle. People asked me how I dealt with my diagnosis and healed my cancer. Here's the thing: I knew I had control over committing to my life and to finding the miracles. I could commit to living as fully as I could. I could commit to meeting me in such a way where I could learn how to be at peace, even in the impossible. A miracle. I don't think for one second that I caused the cancer or healed the cancer. I just chose to commit to life and miracles as long as I was alive.

It took cancer to force me to finally make friends with, and meet, me. A miracle. I will admit that while I had a lot going for me at the time, I didn't know who I was. I repeat, I didn't know who I was. I didn't know what I stood for, really. I almost never thought about what I wanted, just what I should do. I wasn't paying attention to who

I was being. I was focused stubbornly on results and doing instead. I was driven by image and shoulds and thought that as long as every part of my life looked good, I was good. Never let them see you sweat, right? Wrong. Dead wrong. Literally, I almost died. I had twelve surgeries and four months of chemo and a new baby and was stuck in bed for nine months of 2015. During those months I screamed at the top of my lungs. I cried. I couldn't hold my baby because I had tubes coming out of me and my arm wasn't working from multiple surgeries. I felt so alone. But eventually I came home to me. A miracle.

Somehow cancer gave me a voice and more bravery than I knew was in me. A miracle. Man did I fight. A miracle. I became the hero in my story and learned how to trust me. Another miracle. I learned that I didn't need to trust the world, just me. Yet another miracle. What was I going to choose? I became certain that I always have a choice and my voice, in every situation and in every moment. Another miracle.

Cancer was a guarantee that my body, soul, and life were forever changed. A miracle. Nothing was ever going to be the same. Another miracle. My deciding that the rest of my life, would be about what fits in with me. A miracle. It's miraculous that we have our voices and our commitment and our ability to fight for what we want while we are alive. It's miraculous when we allow ourselves to surrender into our emotions.

Your life is yours and it's a miracle. The fear and the freedom that come simultaneously when you realize you can lead and live so that your focus is on what's best for you—a miracle. Your life matters. The beauty that is you has already left a permanent mark on the world. Every moment, breath, and experience has been preparing you to lead in your unique way, as you come back to life and live your comeback story. Use everything that happened or is happening to get closer to who you are. Feel every emotion. Talk. Commit to your life being yours while you connect, heart to heart, to every soul you meet. Live inspired. Inspiration is a willingness to lead in each moment and love with an open heart. Know who you are and what you want. Be all of you. You've never been too much or not enough. Commit to living your most inspired and healed life. Use it all to grow. Be the person you are. Live as much as you can. Lead. Love. Embrace the preciousness that is you while you embrace the preciousness in others.

You have always known who you are. You have never been crazy. You have never been broken. You have always been a force. You came into the world blessed, beautiful, and screaming at the top of your lungs, "I'm alive! I'm here! Do you hear me?" Please be gentle with yourself. Your wounds and judgements won't evaporate overnight. The goal is to take first steps to free yourself up one judgement at a time. The point is to pay attention to what serves you and what doesn't, including your judgements and unhealed wounds. Waiting for other people to stop hurting so that you can stop hurting has to stop. We are all here to serve the planet. We all have a life purpose. When we are willing to heal through past generational patterns, release stuck emotions, and accept support from people, we are available for miracles and get to make our difference. Miracles are there for all of us.

THE HEALING

Now you know how you can use everything that happened or is happening to get closer to who you are and the life you want. Feel every emotion. Talk. Live connected. Heal by creating and living your comeback story. This is how you find your way and break up with survival mode, for good. No more pushing, fighting. Only prepare for miracles. Ease and flow is your birthright. Today can be the beginning of your comeback story. You made it. You survived. Now celebrate!

You have the power to make your life even better than any fantasy you've ever had about what your life could feel like, be like, and look like. It's time for you to tap into faith that life can only get better, because you are only getting better. Have hope that miracles are around every corner, and have the courage to find and take your next right step as your own encourager. No more going through the motions half alive. It's time for you to start living, really living. When you become fully alive, you radiate miracles and inspiration.

You were born hopeful, expecting everything and needing nothing. There was a time when you knew on an unspoken and unconscious level that your needs would always be met. You loved yourself. You trusted yourself. You welcomed fear, anger, grief, excitement, and joy because you wanted to feel fully alive, and you were. You expected miracles. It's time. It's time for you get everything you've ever imagined. You have everything you need. Life is going to get better and better because you are getting better and better.

It's been my honor to take you on this journey of hope and healing. This book is for you, the highly sensitive people who care so much and want to heal the world. It's for the empaths, survivors, caretakers, healers, coaches, parents, leaders, teachers, the game changers, the difference makers, and for the ones who see how life could be. The seminar called your life is waiting for you. We are waiting for you. It's time to begin living from this place. The world needs you healed so you can make your difference. Thank you for being the contribution that you are to humanity. Healing is possible and it starts with you. Thank you for doing your work to live and heal for the world. We need you.

Journal EXERCISE

- What miracles have you experienced as you've read this book?

- What have you learned about yourself after reading this book?

- What is your comeback story?

- Plan a celebration to honor completing this book.

- Every day for the next thirty days, document at least one miracle that you experience in your journal.

- Set a timer and spend ten minutes in front of the mirror honoring your life and the miracle that is you. Then journal about your experience.

Epilogue

Dear Life,

Our journey has been fabulous at times and tragic at times.

But without you, I would be nothing.

With you, I've lived, loved, fallen, risen, and met myself, my purpose, and so many beautiful people.

You've brought me family.

Together we have created joy.

This life is ours for the long game.

I will never be alone because we are in every moment together from this moment forward.

I hear you now.

I see you now.

I respect you now.

I honor you now.

This life has been magnificent for me, only because you have been with me every breath.

Every struggle has been worth it.

Every choice brought lessons and wisdom.

Every moment you continue to teach and guide me.

I choose you now like you've only, always, chosen me.

Love, Rebeccah

Resources

While our goal is that you get what you need from this book, we want to continue to help you heal by offering you additional resources and next-step ideas. Choose from dozens of other options to support you in your continued learning, healing, growth, and success.

- Read this book as many times as you need to.
- Complete the journal questions and use them as many times as you need to.
- Use the tools and processes in this book as many times as you need to.
- Join the Private Healing IS Possible Facebook community here:
  - https://www.facebook.com/groups/Healingispossible
- If you want to go deeper in your work with Rebeccah, there is limited availability for private coaching clients, but she is always accepting applications. You can apply to work with

Rebeccah here: https://www.rebeccahsilence.com/coachin-gapplication (even if there's a wait please know that her team will review your application and will get back to you as soon as possible).

- If therapy is the type of support you want or feel ready for next, you can visit https://www.betterhelp.com/therapists/ to find a therapist who feels like the right fit for you.
- If you want to try Rebeccah's free Three-Step Trauma and Trigger Release Process, visit:
  - https://www.rebeccahsilence.com/trigger-release-method-opt-in
- If you want to go further with Rebeccah's Emotional Survival Kit Course:
  - https://www.rebeccahsilence.com/the-emotional-survival-kit
- If you are a reader and want more book recommendations, here are some of Rebeccah's favorite go to's:
  - *A Course In Miracles*
  - *The Body Keeps the Score*
  - *The Mastery of Love*
  - *The Untethered Soul*
  - *From Tears to Triumph*
  - *You Can Heal Your Life*
  - *Creating a Spiritual Relationship*
  - *High Performance Habits*
  - *Big Magic*
- If you are into podcasts, check out:
  - https://www.lifestough.com/podcast/ tougher-together-breakthrough-podcast/
- If you are a meditator:
  - Download the Insight Timer app.

- If you are into TED Talks:
  - https://www.ted.com/talks/brene_brown_the_power_of_
    vulnerability
  - https://www.ted.com/talks/brene_brown_listening_to_shame
- If you want to go deeper with spirituality:
  - https://livingmiraclescenter.org/livingmiracles/links.html
  - https://www.abraham-hicks.com
  - https://www.lovegrove.club
- If you are into writing, check out:
  - https://club.tut.com/21-day-writing-journey-online
- If you want to try tapping, check out:
  - https://www.thetappingsolution.com
- If you want to join Brendon Burchard's Growth Day:
  - https://www.growthday.com/?via=rebeccah36
- If you want to get support with Judge your Neighbor Work-
  sheets, check out Byron Katie's Helpline for The Work:
  - http://www.instituteforthework.com/itw/content/helpline
- If you are interested in finding out more about Integrative
  Holsitic Coaching and how to become an Integrative Holistic
  Life Coach:
  - https://www.heathersteele.com/IHCCertification
- If you are in need of crisis support:
  - National Suicide Prevention Lifeline, available 24 Hours:
    988
  - National Domestic Violence Hotline, available 24 Hours:
    800-7997233 or Text START TO 88788.

Acknowledgments

This book took four years to birth. It's been a beautiful and messy journey getting here. There are more people to thank than I can mention here but please know that the family members, friends, seminars, co-workers, clients, medical teams, holistic healers, past lovers, support teams, and even strangers that have shared moments of profound connection are in my heart, always. Thank you to everyone who supported me in writing this book. Thank you to everyone who has "seen" me, supported me, and challenged me to live my most healed, honest, and full life in a way that honors the world. I am forever grateful.

To my daughters, be anything that you want to be. You are each more loved and sacred to me than words will ever do justice. To my husband, your love has made all the difference. To my mother, I thank you for your courage in standing by my side as I spread my wings. To Melissa, I love you with all of my heart and am so much better because of all you've taught me. To Holly, my ride or die, how would I do life without you? You are a true best friend and the best of the best. To Annie, thank you for reading as I wrote, and for your honest feedback, friendship, and unmatched support for so many years. To Theresa, you are the best accountability partner there ever was. To my doctors and the team of support that has kept me alive, thank you will never be enough. To Melanie, thank you for your support with the initial manuscript and for believing that there was something here. To my coaches, Carol, Heather S., Eric, Heather B., Dr. Kennedy, Stephen, Brendon, and Dean, you've given me all you have so that I can give all I have, it means so much. To Lisa, my agent, we did it! To Christine and everyone at HCI, this is just the beginning and thank you for seeing and supporting my work. The best is yet to come, for all of us, and healing is possible! Finally, I am thankful for the spiritual crisis of cancer that allowed me to meet, find, and belong to me, God, and the world, again.

About the Author

Rebeccah Silence is a global advocate and leading coach in emotional healing and relationships. As a survivor of childhood trauma and abuse, and being diagnosed with stage 3 cancer while she was pregnant, Rebeccah has successfully led countless individuals, couples, and families to process even the most intense of traumatic experiences—and heal!

An accomplished TV and radio personality with over a decade of experience speaking to millions about doing the inner work, Rebeccah is a groundbreaking voice in the space of healing and self-development. Her life's mission is about supporting people in moving through their healing so that they can allow themselves to truly thrive.

Rebeccah is the author of *Coming Back to Life,* host of the Healing IS Possible Experience and the *Tougher Together Breakthrough* podcast, and the creator of the on-demand Emotional Survival Kit course. Through her coaching, seminars, books, and online courses, Rebeccah teaches us how to become our own healer, how to love and trust ourselves, and how to be our best for others and the world. She currently lives in Boulder, Colorado, with her husband, two daughters, and two dogs.